Prime Time English
Student Book

Contents

Overview of the course

Prime Time English is a language course intended for beginning level students who wish to use English as a language for communication. The goal of *Prime Time English* is to teach students basic communicative language skills, through careful presentation of grammar and vocabulary and through a gradual progression of speaking and listening exercises.

Prime Time English consists of this Student Book, classroom audio cassettes, and a Teacher's Manual. The Student Book contains an Introduction Unit, 12 main units, and Classroom Notes for the teacher. Each of the nine *Presentation Units* (1, 2, 3, 5, 6, 7, 9, 10, 11) presents new grammar points, vocabulary items, listening and speaking exercises, and social exchange formulas. Each of the three *Expansion Units* (4, 8, 12) presents grammar revision exercises and interaction activities.

Organization of the course

The course consists of 12 main units, plus an Introduction Unit. The Classroom Notes, in the back of the textbook for teacher reference, provide additional Warm Up and Follow Up activities. Each of the five sections of a unit requires 30–45 minutes of class time. As such, *Prime Time English* provides a minimum of 36 hours of work. When expansion, review, and self–study activities are utilized, *Prime Time English* provides approximately 48 hours of work.

Introduction Unit

The Introduction Unit provides basic language needed to begin the course. The Introduction Unit gives listening and speaking practice with letters, numbers, colors, clock times, days, months, years, and some helpful classroom expressions.

Presentation Units (1, 2, 3, 5, 6, 7, 9, 10, 11)

Each Presentation Unit contains these sections:

First Try—a presentation of grammar points in short, model conversations and substitution items for practice

Word Bank—a presentation of vocabulary items in a visual context, with a series of exercises to help learn new words

Listening—a set of two types of listening exercises:

   Easy Listening—a series of items to check aural comprehension of new grammar and vocabulary

   Listening Task—a selective listening exercise to develop comprehension of functional language

Pair Practice—an interactive exercise to develop both grammatical accuracy and speaking fluency

Social Talk—a presentation and practice of formulaic language commonly used in social settings

Expansion Units (4, 8, 12)

After every three Presentation Units, there is an Expansion Unit. Each of these units contains exercises for reviewing, consolidating, and expanding the material of the previous lessons. The Expansion Units are intended to be more open than the Presentation Units in order to allow the students to integrate and apply what they have been studying.

Each Expansion Unit contains a combination of these sections:

Grammar Review: These exercises help students review question forms, sentence formation, and word order.

Vocabulary Activities: These exercises help students activate the words and expressions they have been learning.

Interaction Games: These games allow the students to use the language they have studied and enjoy interaction in English.

Classroom Notes

At the back of the book are Classroom Notes for the teacher. These notes give basic classroom procedures for each section of *Prime Time English*. The notes also offer extra Warm Up and Follow Up exercises for each section of every unit so that teachers may challenge their students by expanding the activities of the book. The Classroom Notes are divided into two sections: Teaching Procedures and Unit Notes.

Audio Cassettes

All of the material for the First Try conversation models, Word Bank presentations, Listening exercises, and Social Talk sections are recorded on audio tape. These audio tapes are available separately.

Teacher's Manual

A separate Teacher's Manual contains detailed teaching notes, as well as answer keys for the Student Book exercises, and the Tapescript for the Word Bank and Listening sections.

Basic Tools

1. Letters of the alphabet

Listen and repeat.

A a	B b	C c	D d	E e	F f	G g	H h	I i
J j	K k	L l	M m	N n	O o	P p	Q q	R r
S s	T t	U u	V v	W w	X x	Y y	Z z	

Say these letters.

A	J	K	B	C	D	E	G	P
T	V	Z	I	Y	Q	U	W	F
L	M	N	S	X				

Say your name. Then spell your name.

2. Numbers

Listen and repeat.

1	2	3	4	5	6	7	8	9	10
11	12	13	14	15	16	17	18	19	20
25	30	35	40	45	50	55	60	65	70
75	80	85	90	95	100	150	155	199	200

1,000	1,001	1,019	1,095	1,250	1,791
10,000	10,050	10,555	15,000	18,951	
100,000	100,250	159,777	250,000	750,662	
1,000,000	1,500,000				

1.05	1.1	15.3	15.99	21.063	
$\frac{1}{2}$	$\frac{1}{3}$	$\frac{1}{4}$	$\frac{2}{3}$	$\frac{7}{8}$	$\frac{9}{10}$

Look at these numbers. Say them.

66	72	83	99	101
234	529	667	925	
2,381	44,750	97,852		
150,000	198,250	1,750,000		
6.3	12.45	48.921		
$\frac{5}{6}$	$\frac{1}{7}$	$\frac{9}{10}$		

Say these numbers:

the population of your country   about _____
the population of your city   about _____

3. Colors

Listen and repeat.

Basic colors:

white	black	gray	brown	red
orange	yellow	green	blue	pink

Other colors:

light blue	light green	dark blue	dark green	silver	gold

What color is it? Say the color.

4. Time

Listen and repeat.

7:00	7:15	7:30	7:45 a.m.	7:50 p.m.
12:00 noon		12:00 midnight		

What time is it? Say the time.

5. Days and months

Listen and repeat.

Sunday   Monday   Tuesday   Wednesday   Thursday   Friday   Saturday

Listen and repeat.

January	February	March	April	May	June
July	August	September	October	November	December

6. Years

Listen and repeat.

1970	Nineteen seventy		1993	Nineteen ninety-three
1979	Nineteen seventy-nine		2000	Two thousand
1990	Nineteen ninety		2010	Twenty ten

Say the year.

1925   1941   1952   1963   1977   1980   1992   1999

7. Dates 📼

Listen and repeat.

Monday, January 15th, 1992
Wednesday, August 1st, 1975
Friday, December 3rd, 1982
Sunday, December 31st, 1999

Say these dates.

8. Directions 📼

Listen and repeat.

in   on   under   next to   to the right of   to the left of   in the middle
at the top of   at the bottom of   in the top-right corner
in the bottom-left corner

Describe these pictures.

9. Classroom expressions 📼

Listen and repeat.

Sorry. I don't understand.
Could you say that again, please?
Please repeat that.

Did you say ...?
Do you mean ...?
Does that mean ...?

What does ... mean?
What does it mean?
Do you know what I mean?

Excuse me. I have a question.
How do you pronounce that?
How do you spell that?

How do you say ... in English?
What's this in English?
What do you call that in English?

What's this?
Sorry, I don't know.

Let me try that again.

First Try

1. Pronunciation

Listen and repeat.

> Do you live in New York?   Do you work in Chicago?   What do you do?
> I live on 14th Street.   Yes, I work at the Sears Building.   Do you like your job?

2. Just listen

Listen to the conversations.

1.

Hello, I'm Mark Horner.
(your name)
Hi, I'm Jill Ohara.
(your partner's name)
Do you live in New York?
(your city)
Yes, I do. I live on 14th Street.
(your street)
How about you?
I live on 21st Street.
(your partner's street)

2.

Hello, I'm Sally Davis.
(name)
Hi, I'm Gwen Wong.
(name)
Do you work in Chicago?
(city)
Yes, I work at the Sears Building.
(place)
How about you?
I work at the AT&T Building.
(place)

3.

What do you do?
I'm a nurse.
(job)
I work at Waverly Hospital.
(place)
Oh really? Do you like it there?
Yes, of course.
Yes, I love it!

4.

What do you do?
I'm a lawyer.
(job)
I work for Marks and Sanders.
(company name)
Do you like your job?
No, not really.
No, I hate it!

3. Work in pairs

Practice the conversations. Then practice again. Use the new words and phrases.

1

Word Bank 🔊

Listen and look at the pictures. Repeat the words and phrases.

Daily activities

get dressed

brush my teeth

comb my hair

put on make-up

shave

wash my face

type letters

use a computer

do the dishes

exercise

stay up late

go to meetings

Interests

swimming

theater

languages

knitting

going to
music clubs

cycling

playing sports
(golf)

watching
sports

1. Do you like it?

Ask your partner this question: Do you like (skiing)?
Make a check (✓) in one column for each activity.

	love it	really like it	like it a little (It's OK.)	don't like it	hate it	don't know (never tried it)
skiing						
driving						
swimming						
cycling						
hiking						
ice skating						

2. How often do you …?

Ask your partner this question: How often do you (brush your teeth)?
Make a check (✓) in one column for each activity.

Daily Activities	do it every day	do it most days	do it some days	never do it
brush your teeth				
put on make-up				
wash your hair				
stay up late				
drink coffee				

3. What time?

What time do you usually do these things? Write a time for each action. Then ask your partner.

	Time		**Time**
wake up	_____	have lunch	_____
eat breakfast	_____	have dinner	_____
leave home for school or work	_____	go to bed	_____

Now answer these questions.

What do you usually do in the evenings? _____

What do you usually do on the weekends? _____

New Words
Do you know more words?

Daily activities

Interests

_____   _____

_____   _____

Listening

1. Easy listening

Listen. Check (✓) the job.

teacher ❑

government worker ❑

taxi driver ❑

entertainer ❑

newscaster ❑

coach ❑

loan officer ❑

farmer ❑

architect ❑

Listen. Check (✓) the actions.

teach high school
math ❏

work in a
government office ❏

drive a
taxi ❏

sing in
music clubs ❏

announce the
news ❏

coach a
basketball team ❏

work at a bank ❏

grow vegetables ❏

design buildings ❏

2. Listening task

Listen. Fill in this form.

Job Application

Happy Day Child Care Center

name ....
date of birth ....
current job ....
previous jobs ....
....
interests ....
....

Pair Practice A

Student A look at this page. Student B look at page 8.

Ask your partner about 1, 3, 5, 7, 9. Ask this question:

What does (Laura Mayer) do?

Write the answers. Take turns. Answer B's questions about 2, 4, 6, 8, 10.

1. Laura Mayer
   _____

2. Martin Swartz
   musician

3. Ahmed Al-Shaye
   _____

4. Leona Hinton
   doctor

5. Ronald Lin
   _____

6. Anita Wilson
   lawyer

7. Gary Morrison
   _____

8. K.J. Kim
   flight attendant

9. Pedro Martinez
   _____

10. Pietro Zanghi
    writer

• •

EXTRA! EXTRA!

Famous People

*Work with your partner.
How many of these people
do you recognize?
What are their names?
What do they do?*

I think number (1) is .... He/She's a ....

1

2

3

4

5

Social Talk—Introductions

1. Listen in

Listen to the conversations.

1.

Hi, Mari.

Hi, Richard. Richard, I'd like you to meet Jason.

Hi, Jason. Glad to meet you.

Glad to meet you too, Richard.

2.

Mom, this is Nathan. Nathan, this is my mom.

Oh, hello, Nathan. Glad to meet you.

Glad to meet you too, Mrs. Stratton.

3.

Hi, Mike. Who's your friend?

Oh, let me introduce you. Lynn, this is Susan. Susan, Lynn.

Nice to meet you, Lynn.

Nice to meet you, Susan.

4.

I'd like to introduce my friend, Peter.

Oh, hello, Peter. Glad to meet you. I'm Steve.

Hello, Steve. Glad to meet you too.

2. Act it out

Work with two partners. Stand up. Act out the conversations.
Then make your own conversations. Use your own words and ideas.

Pair Practice B 👥

Student B look at this page. Student A look at page 6.

Ask your partner about 2, 4, 6, 8, 10. Ask this question:

What does (Martin Swartz) do?

Write the answers. Take turns. Answer A's questions about 1, 3, 5, 7, 9.

1. Laura Mayer
   police officer

2. Martin Swartz
   _____

3. Ahmed Al-Shaye
   translator

4. Leona Hinton
   _____

5. Ronald Lin
   athlete

6. Anita Wilson
   _____

7. Gary Morrison
   tour guide

8. K.J. Kim
   _____

9. Pedro Martinez
   photographer

10. Pietro Zanghi
    _____

- -

EXTRA! EXTRA! 👥

Famous People

*Work with your partner.
How many of these people
do you recognize?
What are their names?
What do they do?*

1

2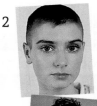

3

4

5

I think number (1) is .... He/She's a ....

First Try

1. Pronunciation 📼

Listen and repeat.

> Do you know Tom?   What's he wearing?   What does he look like?
> He's wearing a black jacket.   He's very tall and thin.
> He's standing next to the door.

2. Just listen 📼

Listen to the conversations.

1.

Do you know Tom Nakano?
(name)
I don't think so. What does he look like?
He's about 25 years old.
(age)
And he's very tall and thin.
short and heavy
Oh, yes, I know him.

2.

Do you know Annie and Alice?
(names)
I'm not sure. What do they look like?
They're about 15 years old.
(age)
Annie is tall and Alice is short.
very tall   very short
Oh, yes, I know them.

3.

Do you see Jack?
No, I don't. What's he wearing ?
He's wearing a black jacket.
(clothes item)
Oh, yes, I see him.

4.

Do you see Jackie?
Yes, she's over there.
Where?
She's standing next to the door.
(place)
She's talking to Paul.
(doing something)
Oh, yes, I see her.

3. Work in pairs 👥

Practice the conversations. Then practice again. Use the new words and phrases.

2

Word Bank

Listen and look at the pictures. Repeat the words and phrases.

Clothes

1. blue jeans
2. hat
3. glasses
4. blouse
5. shirt
6. dress
7. purse
8. shoulder bag
9. skirt
10. shoes
11. socks
12. sweatshirt
13. sneakers
14. T-shirt
15. suit

wallet   earrings   ring   necklace   bracelet   watch

Hair

long hair   short hair   curly hair   straight hair   dark hair   light hair

Body type

short   tall   average height   slim   medium build   heavy

1. That's a nice...

Work with a partner. Look at each picture. Take turns.

Say: That's a nice (dress).   Those are nice (shoes).
Answer: Thanks.

1.

2.

3.

4.

5.

2. He's...

Look at each picture. Describe the people.

1.

He has *short* hair.
He's wearing

_____.

He looks like a/an

_____ person.

2.

She has _____ hair.
She's wearing

_____.

She looks like a/an

_____ person.

3.

He has _____ hair.
He's wearing

_____.

He looks like a/an

_____ person.

3. In this class

Work with a partner. Ask and answer.

Is anyone wearing (a red sweater)? Who?

Ask about these items:

a red sweater   a funny T-shirt   white sneakers   white socks   long earrings
a white bracelet   a gold ring   blue jeans   a gray sweatshirt   blue shoes
black glasses   a striped shirt   a silver watch   a tie

New Words
Do you know more words?

_____

Listening

1. Easy listening

Listen. Which people? Check (✓) the pictures.

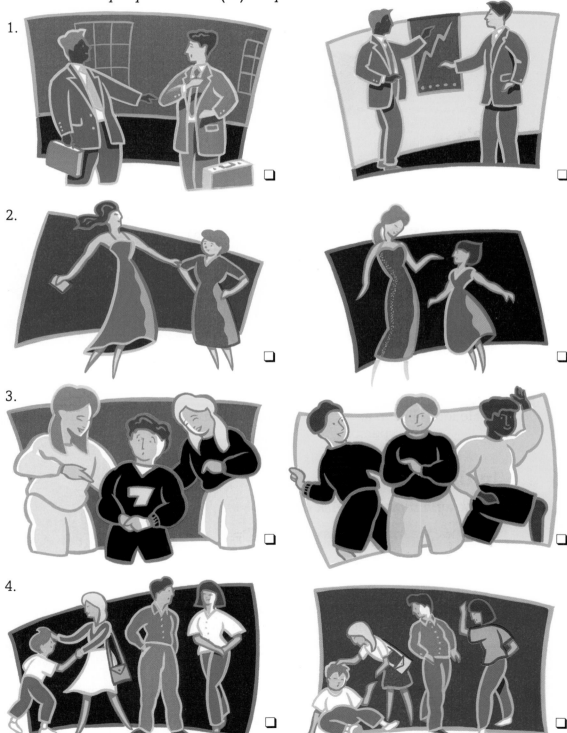

1.

2.

3.

4.

2. Listening task

Draw a line from the names to the people in the picture.

1. Mark   Alexander   Jesse

2. Luisa   Miguel   Elena   Maria

3. Keiichi Eri Eiji Kimiko Emiko Toshi Masa

Pair Practice A

Student A look at this page. Student B look at page 16.

Your partner has a different picture. How many differences can you find?

Take turns. Ask these questions:

> Who is (on the left)?
> What is (he) wearing?

Describe your picture:

> In my picture, (the father) is on the left. (He) is wearing (a black shirt).

What are the differences?

father   older brother

_____   _____

older sister   mother

_____   _____

younger brother   younger sister

_____   _____

· ·

EXTRA! EXTRA!

Who is it?

Work with a partner. Turn your back to the room.
Your partner will ask ten questions.

> Is there a (map) in the room?
> Is there a person wearing (a red tie) in the room?
>
> Who is next to (*name*)?   Who is in front of (*name*)?

Then change roles. Who can answer the most questions?

Social Talk—Responses

1. Listen in

Listen to the conversations.

1.
> What do you think of our new teacher?
>
> Oh, he's great. I really like him.

2.
> What did you think of the concert?
>
> I thought it was fantastic!

3.
> What did you think of the movie?
>
> Oh, it was just so-so. I didn't really like it.

4.
> Meg, this salad is great!
>
> Thanks. I'm glad you like it.

2. Act it out

Work with a partner. Stand up. Act out the conversations. Then make your own conversations. Use your own words and ideas.

Pair Practice B

Student B look at this page. Student A look at page 14.

Your partner has a different picture. How many differences can you find?

Take turns. Ask these questions:

> Who is (on the right)?
> What is (he) wearing?

Describe your picture:

> In my picture, (the father) is on the right. (He) is wearing (a white shirt).

What are the differences?

father

_____

older sister

_____

younger brother

_____

older brother

_____

mother

_____

younger sister

_____

• •

EXTRA! EXTRA!

Who is it?

Work with a partner. Turn your back to the room. Your partner will ask ten questions.

> Is there a (map) in the room?
> Is there a person wearing (a red tie) in the room?
>
> Who is next to (*name*)?   Who is in front of (*name*)?

Then change roles. Who can answer the most questions?

UNIT THREE
First Try

1. Pronunciation

Listen and repeat.

> How was your English test?   Hey, that's terrific.   Oh, that's too bad.
> I'm glad to hear that.   I'm sorry to hear that.

2. Just listen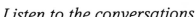

Listen to the conversations.

1.

How was your English test yesterday?
Math test

Great. I got an A.
got 95%

Hey, that's terrific! I'm glad to
hear that.

2.

How was the game last night?
the match

Not so good. We lost—55 to 10.
We got beat—95 to 2.

Oh, that's too bad. I'm sorry to
hear that.

3.

How was your shopping trip this
morning?
Great. I bought some new clothes.
I got some sports equipment.
Oh, good. I'm glad to hear that.

4.

How was your date last night?
Not so good.
Paul and I had an argument.
We had a fight.
Oh, that's too bad. I'm sorry to
hear that.

3. Work in pairs

*Practice the conversations. Then practice again. Use the new words
and phrases.*

Word Bank 📼

Listen and look at the pictures. Repeat the words and phrases.

Actions

(see) saw a movie

(do) did my homework

(buy) bought something

(borrow) borrowed some money

(move) moved to a new apartment

(take) took a trip

(get) got a haircut

(have) had a date with someone

Emotions

angry

excited

disappointed

nervous

sorry

tired

upset

surprised

Time expressions

on Friday night   last night   yesterday   last week   last month   last year

1. Yes, I did.

Work with a partner. Ask and answer.

Did you (go to a restaurant) yesterday?   Yes, I did. *or* No, I didn't.

Choose five questions.

- go to a restaurant
- buy a newspaper
- stay up late
- get angry at someone
- watch a good TV program
- visit a friend
- meet someone new
- cook your own dinner
- do your English homework
- see something unusual

Ask two more questions.

2. When was the last time?

Work with a partner. Ask and answer.

When was the last time that you (went to a birthday party)?
Last week. (*or* Last month *or* Two years ago)

Choose five questions.

- held a baby?
- saw a sports match?
- bought something expensive?
- had dinner with your father?
- did your English homework?
- went on a holiday trip?
- received a nice gift?
- took an important test?
- wrote a letter?

Ask two more questions.

3. How did they feel?

Look at the pictures. Complete each sentence.

1. He was _____ when he read the letter.

2. She was _____ when she heard the news.

3. He was _____ when she called him.

4. She was _____ when he left the room.

5. He was _____ when he broke the window.

6. They were _____ when they took the test.

7. We were _____ after we ran in the race.

8. I was _____ when I saw my score on the test.

New Words

Do you know more words?

Activities

Interests

_____   _____

Listening

1. Easy listening

Listen. Check (✓) the correct picture.

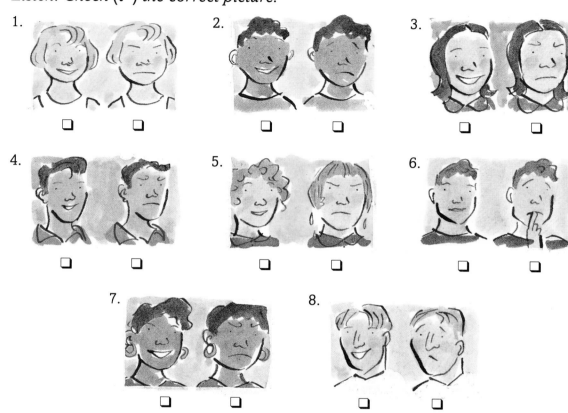

1.   ❏   ❏

2.   ❏   ❏

3.   ❏   ❏

4.   ❏   ❏

5.   ❏   ❏

6.   ❏   ❏

7.   ❏   ❏

8.   ❏   ❏

Check (✓) the correct picture.

1.   ❏   ❏

2.   ❏   ❏

3.   ❏   ❏

4.   ❏   ❏

5.   ❏   ❏

6.   ❏   ❏

2. Listening task

Listen. Complete the postcards.

Dear Paul and Sue,
I'm _____ a great time here in
Hawaii. _____ warm and
_____ today, but yesterday
_____ rainy and
_____ . On Sunday, I
_____ wind surfing.
I _____ a great time!
Tomorrow, I'm _____
_____ deep sea
fishing. I'm _____
and _____ myself.
I wish you were with me.
Take care,
       Ted

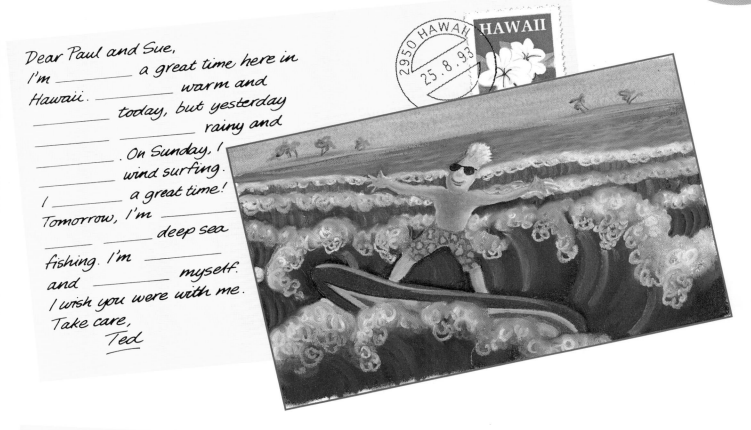

Dear Gina and Howie,
I just _____ in Switzerland. I
_____ a _____ time because
my flight _____ delayed two
times and I _____ my carry-on
bag with my money and my passport
in the London airport. It _____
_____ ! Someone _____ my
bag, but my money _____
gone. A friend _____
me some money. Anyway,
_____ OK now. It's
beautiful here. The weather
here is very _____ and
there's a lot of snow, but the
sky is _____ and blue.
I'll write more later.
       Love,
         Lisa

Pair Practice A 👥

Student A look at this page. Student B look at page 24.

Your partner has different information. Fill in the missing information. Ask your partner this question about 2, 4, 6, 8:

What did (Peter Jones) do (yesterday)?

Take turns. Answer your partner's questions about 1, 3, 5, 7.

1. Sandy Wilson went to the beach

2. Peter Jones
   _____
   _____

3. The Hendersons had a barbecue party

4. Risa Kondoh
   _____
   _____

5. Melissa and Harry took a drive

6. Peter Murphy
   _____
   _____

7. Vanna Green went to the dentist

8. Eddie Chen
   _____
   _____

. . . .

EXTRA! EXTRA! 👥

Past Actions

Work with your partner. Find three things that both you and your partner did yesterday. Ask your partner:

Did you (buy some clothes) yesterday?
or What is one thing you did between (6 and 7 p.m.)?

Social Talk—Events

3

1. Listen in

Listen to the conversations.

1.
> Hi, Margie. Where are you going?
>
> I'm going to class. I've got to take an English test.
>
> Good luck.
>
> Thanks.

2.

> Are you going somewhere?
>
> Yeah, I'm going skiing this weekend.
>
> That sounds like fun. Have a good time.
>
> Thanks.

3.

> Hi, Mick. What's up?
>
> I'm going to visit Lucy in the hospital.
>
> Well, give her my best.
>
> OK, I will.

4.

> Hi, Ted. Where are you off to?
>
> I'm going home. I've got to study.
>
> OK, see you later.
>
> Bye.

2. Act it out

Work with a partner. Stand up. Act out the conversations.
Then make your own conversations. Use your own words and ideas.

Pair Practice B

Student B look at this page. Student A look at page 22.

Your partner has different information. Fill in the missing information. Ask your partner this question about 1, 3, 5, 7:

What did (Sandy Wilson) do (yesterday)?

Take turns. Answer your partner's questions about 2, 4, 6, 8.

1. Sandy Wilson
   _____
   _____

2. Peter Jones
   got a haircut

3. The Hendersons
   _____
   _____

4. Risa Kondoh
   went to the
   hospital

5. Melissa and
   Harry _____
   _____

6. Peter Murphy
   wrote some
   letters

7. Vanna Green
   _____
   _____

8. Eddie Chen
   bought some
   new clothes

• •

EXTRA! EXTRA!

Past Actions

Work with your partner. Find three things that both you and your partner did yesterday. Ask your partner:

Did you (buy some clothes) yesterday?
or What is one thing you did between (6 and 7 p.m.)?

Expansion Unit

1   **1. Questions and Answers**

Match each answer with a question.

Answers	Questions
About an hour.	Do you have any brothers or sisters?
At home.	Where are you going?
Coffee and eggs.	What's the matter?
During our summer vacation.	How long did you wait for me?
Great.	Did you invite her to the party?
I lost my wallet.	When did you visit Greece?
I'm twenty-one.	How was your meeting yesterday?
Jeans and a green sweater.	What is she wearing?
No, I didn't. I forgot.	Where were you last night?
No, I don't.	What did you have for breakfast?
Three – me and my parents.	How many people are there in your family?
To school.	How old are you?

2. Grammar Watch

Check (✓) the correct sentence, A or B. Circle the error.

A	**B**
1. Do you have a brothers or sisters?	Do you have any brothers or sisters?
2. Do you have a car?	Do you have car?
3. Where you going?	Where are you going?
4. What you do in your free time?	What do you do in your free time?
5. Where do you work?	Where do you working?
6. He live on 21st Street.	He lives on 21st Street.
7. She's very tall.	She very tall.
8. There he is. He wears a black jacket.	There he is. He's wearing a black jacket.
9. Last week I bought some clothes.	Last week I buy some clothes.
10. How was your test yesterday?	How is your test yesterday?
11. What you did last night?	What did you do last night?
12. They were sad when they heard the news.	They were sad when they hear the news.

3. Description

Work in pairs. Take turns to describe each picture.
Say at least three sentences about each.

There is a ...	(The man) is (do)ing ...
There are ...	(The woman) is wearing ...

1.

2.

3.

4.

5.

6.

4. Vocabulary Exercise—Categories

Work with a partner. Ask and answer.

Which one doesn't belong?
(Tie) doesn't belong.

1. shirt	sweater	trousers	earrings
2. get dressed	wash your hair	take a bath	take a shower
3. ring	earrings	tie	necklace
4. go to a meeting	brush your teeth	write a report	type a letter
5. swimming	listening to music	doing housework	playing sports
6. striped	solid	big	checked
7. friendly	nice	interesting	tall
8. last night	tomorrow	yesterday	last year
9. yesterday	tomorrow	next week	next year
10. tall	young	slim	heavy

5. Vocabulary Expansion

Think of:

1. Three things that are green

   _____ _____ _____

2. Three things you wear in cold weather

   _____ _____ _____

3. Two bright colors

   _____ _____

4. Four activities you can do at home

   _____ _____ _____ _____

5. Five sports you can do in the summer

   _____ _____ _____ _____ _____

6. Five activities you do every day

   _____ _____ _____ _____ _____

7. Four jobs people do in offices

   _____ _____ _____ _____

8. Two adjectives to describe people's body type

   _____ _____

9. Four words to describe the weather

   _____ _____ _____ _____

10. Two places to go at night for entertainment

   _____ _____

6. Activities—One-minute pantomime

Two students work together. Plan a one–minute skit with no words, only action. Act it out. Here are some themes:

- Party
- Trip
- Riding the bus
- Office work
- Buying a train ticket

Other students watch. Then they recall and tell the skit using the past tense.

First, a man got on the bus and sat down. Then a woman got on the bus. She had a lot of packages. The man stood up. She dropped all of her packages...

First Try

1. Pronunciation 🔲

Listen and repeat.

| Do we need any bread?   Where is it?   Do we need any apples? |
| It's in the back of the store.   How many do we need? |

2. Just listen 🔲

Listen to the conversations.

1.

Do we need any bread?
milk

No, we don't.
How about rice?
cheese
We don't have any. We'd better buy some.

2.

Do we need any apples?
oranges

Yes, we do.
How many should I get?
Four or five.
About ten.

3.

Do you sell yogurt?
soft drinks

Yes, we do.
Where is it?
are they
It's in the dairy section at the back of
They're
the store.

4.

Do you have any brown rice?
cream cheese

Yes, we do. It's in Aisle 6.
Aisle 6?
Yes, it's next to the pasta.
butter

3. Work in pairs 👥

Practice the conversations. Then practice again. Use the new words and phrases.

Word Bank

Buying things

Listen and look at the pictures. Repeat the words and phrases.

How many ...s?

cookies   onions   apples   eggs

6 cookies
2 onions
3 kilos of apples
12 eggs

How much ...?

rice   milk   butter   cheese

2 kilos of rice
$1/4$ kilo of butter
1 kilo of cheese
3 liters of milk

Containers

a bag of...
rice

a bottle of...
ketchup, soy sauce,
wine

a box of...
tissue paper,
crackers

a can of...
tomato soup,
soda, beer

a carton of...
eggs

a container of...
yogurt, cream,
butter

a jar of...
peanut butter,
mayonnaise

a package of...
cookies, cream
cheese

Types of stores

supermarket

drug store

book store

stationery store

department store

hardware store

electronics
store

bakery

1. Do we have any?

Work with a partner. Ask and answer.

> Do we have any (bread)?
> Yes, we do. We have (one loaf).
> *or* No, we don't. We don't have any.

1. bread	2. oranges
3. eggs	4. milk
5. cookies	6. peanut butter
7. cheese	8. soy sauce

2. Let's make a ...

Work with a partner. Make conversations.

> Let's make (an omelette).   We can't. There aren't any (eggs).
>   *or* We don't have any (eggs).
>
> Let's make (a pizza).   We can't. There isn't any (cheese).
>   *or* We don't have any (cheese).

1. sandwich/bread	2. orange juice/oranges	3. apple pie/apples
4. tempura/flour	5. salsa/tomatoes	6. pizza/cheese
7. kimchi/cabbage	8. jambalaya/rice	9. omelette/eggs

3. Excuse me. Do you sell ...?

Where can you buy these items? Write the type of store next to each item.
Then make short conversations with a partner.

> Excuse me. Do you sell (cameras)?
> *or* Do you have any (cameras)?   Yes, we do. They're over there.
>
> Excuse me. Do you sell (shampoo)?
> *or* Do you have any (shampoo)?   Yes, we do. It's over there.

	Type of store		**Type of store**
1. running shoes	_____	2. coffee beans	_____
3. paint	_____	4. magazines	_____
5. shampoo	_____	6. envelopes	_____
7. cosmetics	_____	8. cameras	_____

New Words

Do you know more words?

Things	**Containers**	**Places**
_____	_____	_____

Listening

5

1. Easy listening

What did they buy? Check (✓) the items.

Listen and write the quantities.

1. _____ of beef, _____ of chicken,
   _____ of fish.

2. _____ of orange soda,
   _____ grapefruit juice.

3. _____ eggs and _____ bread.

4. _____ chocolate chip cookies,
   _____ potato chips, _____ peanuts.

5. _____ tomato soup, _____ soy sauce,
   _____ rice.

Listen and write the prices.

1. gold pen _____

   silver pen _____

2. repair the TV _____

3. antique mirror _____

4. car _____

5. grapes _____/kilo

6. chair: sale price _____

   regular price _____

2. Listening task

Listen. Where does each conversation take place?
Number the stores correctly.

Pair Practice A

Student A look at this page. Student B look at page 36.

Ask your partner about the prices at his or her shopping mall. Write the price. Find the best price for each item and circle it. Ask this question:

What's the price of (a six-pack of Jolt-Plus cola) at Shopper City Mall?

Answer your partner's questions.

Your shopping list:	price at Super Mall	price at Shopper City Mall
a Sonic 36-inch TV	$550	_____
a six-pack of Jolt-Plus Cola	$4	_____
a bottle of Napa Red wine	$12	_____
a copy of *Mystery at Sea*	$21	_____
a pair of On Air running shoes	$98	_____
a kilo of Kenya coffee beans	$18	_____
Elena Jackson's new CD	$20	_____

EXTRA! EXTRA!

What's in the package?

Work with a partner. Ask and answer. Take turns.

What do you think number (1) is?   I think number (1) is...

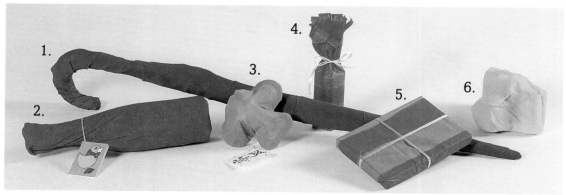

Social Talk—Shopping

1. Listen in

Listen to the conversations.

1.

Can I help you?

No, thanks. I'm just looking.

2.

Excuse me. Do you sell electric appliances?

Yes, we do. They're on the 4th floor.

Thank you.

You're welcome.

3.

How much is this skirt?

It's $99. Would you like to try it on?

Yes, I would.

The dressing rooms are over there.

4.

Can I take your order?

Yes, I'd like some vegetable soup and a large iced tea.

Anything else?

No, that's all.

2. Act it out

Work with a partner. Stand up. Act out the conversations.
Then make your own conversations. Use your own words and ideas.

Pair Practice B

Student B look at this page. Student A look at page 34.

Ask your partner about the prices at his or her shopping mall. Write the price. Find the best price for each item and circle it. Ask this question:

What's the price of (a six-pack of Jolt-Plus cola) at Super Mall?

Answer your partner's questions.

Your shopping list:	price at Super Mall	price at Shopper City Mall
a Sonic 36-inch TV	_____	$595
a six-pack of Jolt-Plus cola	_____	$5
a bottle of Napa Red wine	_____	$10
a copy of Mystery at Sea	_____	$18
a pair of On Air running shoes	_____	$88
a kilo of Kenya coffee beans	_____	$19
Elena Jackson's new CD	_____	$20

• •

EXTRA! EXTRA!

What's in the package?

Work with a partner. Ask and answer. Take turns.

What do you think number (1) is?   I think number (1) is...

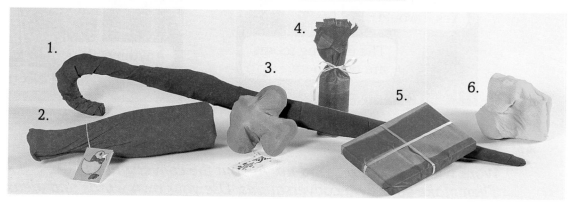

First Try

1. Pronunciation

Listen and repeat.

> What are you going to do tonight?   I'm going to a party.
> What are you going to do this weekend?   I'm going to visit my relatives.
> What are you planning to do this summer?

2. Just listen

Listen to the conversations.

1.

What are you going to do tonight?
I'm going to go to Chaco's party.
                    a reception
Chaco's party? Where is it?
A reception?
It's at her house.
                    the Hilton Hotel

2.

What are you going to do this weekend?
I'm going to go to Lake Tahoe.
                    Mt. Lava
Lake Tahoe? Where's that?
Mt. Lava
It's in Northern California.
                    Orange County

3.

What are you going to do this weekend?
On Saturday, I'm going to
            I'll probably
work in my garden.
How about on Sunday?
On Sunday, I'm going to
            I might
visit my relatives.

4.

What are you planning
                going
to do this summer?
In July, I'm planning to
            going to
travel in Europe.
Oh, really? How about in August?
In August, I'm going to study in the States.

3. Work in pairs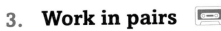

Practice the conversations. Then practice again. Use the new words and phrases.

Word Bank 📼

Listen and look at the pictures. Repeat the words and phrases.

Places in a city

post office

bank

park

hospital

movie theater

campus

library

school

train station

bus station

bus stop

hairdresser

Places in the countryside

town

mountain

lake

river

Directions

north, south, east, west

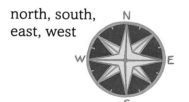

on the right

on the left

near   next to   off of (Oxford Street)

1. Where are you going?

Work in pairs. Ask and answer. Take turns.

> Where are you going?   I'm going to (the post office).
> What are you going to do there?   I'm going to (mail a letter).

1. post office – mail a letter
2. park – take a nap
3. hairdresser – have my hair cut
4. movie theater – see a movie
5. campus – go to a class
6. bank – cash a check
7. library – borrow some books
8. bus stop – catch the bus
9. hospital – visit one of my relatives
10. airport – fly to Los Angeles

2. Where is it?

Work in pairs. Ask and answer. Take turns.

> Where is (the train station)?   It's (on, in, at, near) (Murray Street).

1. Berkeley – San Francisco
2. the train station – Murray Street
3. The Amazon River – South America
4. Moe's Bookstore – the university
5. the stadium – Oakland
6. Mt. Fuji – central Japan

3. How do I get there?

Work in pairs. Look at the map. Ask and answer these questions. Take turns.

> How can I get to
> (Lake Tamako)?
> It's (north). Take
> (Highway 4) to
> (Lake Road).

1. Lake Tamako
2. The Capitol Building
3. Mt. Shasta
4. Central State University
5. The Rockies Stadium

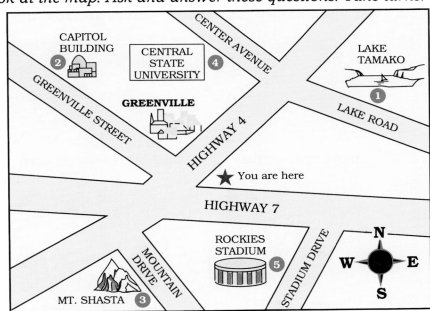

New Words

Do you know more words?

Places

Directions

_____

_____

Listening

6

1. Easy listening

Check (✓) the phrase you hear.

- ❏ soon
- ❏ after you graduate
- ❏ before work
- ❏ when I come back from my vacation
- ❏ during summer vacation

- ❏ I don't know
- ❏ after I get home
- ❏ after I get married
- ❏ tomorrow
- ❏ next month
- ❏ never

- ❏ after school
- ❏ after work
- ❏ before class
- ❏ next weekend
- ❏ the day after tomorrow

Check (✓) the actions you hear.

go on a diet ❏

study abroad ❏

write a book ❏

move to Australia ❏

take care of my children ❏

have a family ❏

get a job ❏

have an interview ❏

go on vacation ❏

take it easy ❏

go surfing ❏

watch the sunset ❏

2. Listening task 🔲

Listen. Put the actions in order. Number the pictures.

spend a week with my sister in New York ❑

go to Japan for my friend's wedding ❑

work at a department store to make some money ❑

spend a couple of weeks with my parents in Florida ❑

Pair Practice A

Student A look at this page. Student B look at page 44.

Your partner has different information. Fill in the missing information. Ask this question about 1, 3, 5, 7:

What is (Ahmed) going to do (on Sunday afternoon)?

Take turns. Answer your partner's questions about 2, 4, 6, 8.

1. Ahmed
   Sunday afternoon
   _____
   _____

2. Mr. Choy
   this Saturday
   work in his garden

3. Lucia and Emilio
   during their winter break
   _____
   _____

4. Erica
   this summer
   go to language
   school in the USA

5. Eva
   after she wakes up
   _____
   _____

6. Erik
   after he graduates
   work at a bank

7. Tony and Yvonne
   after dinner
   _____
   _____

8. Mr. and Mrs. Smith
   during their vacation
   visit their son

EXTRA! EXTRA!

Fortune Teller

Work with a partner. Make predictions about his/her future. Tell your partner one prediction for each topic:

love   marriage   family   place to live   future job   future travel
future success

I think you're going to (travel round the world).

Listen to your partner's predictions about you. Do you think they will happen?

Social Talk—Invitations

1. Listen in

Listen to the conversations.

1.

2.

3.

4.

2. Act it out

Work with a partner. Stand up. Act out the conversations. Then make your own conversations. Use your own words and ideas.

Pair Practice B

Student B look at this page. Student A look at page 42.

Your partner has different information. Fill in the missing information. Ask this question about 2, 4, 6, 8:

What is (Mr Choy) going to do (this Saturday)?

Take turns. Answer your partner's questions about 1, 3, 5, 7.

1. Ahmed
   Sunday afternoon
   do his laundry

2. Mr. Choy
   this Saturday
   _____
   _____

3. Lucia and Emilio
   during their winter break
   ski in Colorado

4. Erica
   this summer
   _____
   _____

5. Eva
   after she wakes up
   make coffee

6. Erik
   after he graduates
   _____
   _____

7. Tony and Yvonne
   after dinner
   take a walk

8. Mr. and Mrs. Smith
   during their vacation
   _____
   _____

• •

EXTRA! EXTRA!

Fortune Teller

Work with a partner. Make predictions about his/her future. Tell your partner one prediction for each topic:

love   marriage   family   place to live   future job   future travel
future success

I think you're going to (travel round the world).

Listen to your partner's predictions about you. Do you think they will happen?

First Try

1. Pronunciation

Listen and repeat.

> Do you want to go to a movie tonight?   No, sorry, I can't. I have to work tonight.   Could you carry this for me?   Sure. No problem.

2. Just listen

Listen to the conversations.

1.

Do you want to go to a movie tonight?
a concert
I can't. I have to work late tonight.
study
How about on Saturday?
Sunday
Sure, I can go then.

2.

Do you want to go camping
go surfing
this weekend?
*No, sorry, I can't. I have to
go on a business trip this weekend.*
take care of my kids
How about next weekend?
Sure, I can go then.

3.

Can you help me?
give me a hand
Sure. What is it?
Could you carry this for me?
hold this
I have a sore back.
sore shoulder
OK. No problem.

4.

Mary, can you help me?
do me a favor
Sure, if I can. What is it?
Could you take me to the doctor's
drive
office? I have a fever.
sore shoulder
Sure. I'll be right there.

3. Work in pairs

Practice the conversations. Then practice again. Use the new words and phrases.

Word Bank 📼

Health

Listen and look at the pictures. Repeat the words and phrases.

Health problems
have ...
1. a headache
   a toothache
2. a stomachache
   an earache
3. a sore back
   a sore throat
   a sore shoulder
4. a cold
   a cough
   an infection
5. a cut
6. a burn
7. a broken bone
   (arm wrist finger
   leg ankle toe)
   a sprain

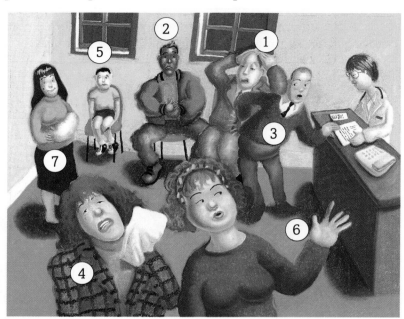

Health care
1. cough medicine
2. stomach medicine
3. vitamins
4. aspirin
5. cold medicine

health foods  junk food

gain weight   lose weight   get some exercise   go on a diet

Adjectives

tired   hungry   thirsty   sunburned

1. I'm sorry to hear that!

Work with a partner. Take turns. Look at the large picture on page 46.

Say: I have a (headache).   *Answer:* Oh, I'm sorry to hear that.

2. You might...

What might happen? Complete each sentence.

1. If you don't sleep enough, you might get _____.
2. If you eat too much sweet food, you might get _____.
3. If you lift too many heavy things, you might get _____.
4. If you eat too much rich food, you might get _____.
5. If you stay outside in rainy weather, you might get _____.
6. If you shout too much, you might get _____.
7. If you play with a knife, you might get _____.
8. If you _____, you might get _____.
   (your own idea)

3. Maybe you should...

Read each sentence. Find the right advice.

I'm tired.   Why don't you do something?
I'm hungry.   Why don't you lie down?
I'm thirsty.   You'd better not lift anything.
My hair is too long.   Why don't you eat health foods?
My hair is dirty.   You'd better visit the dentist.
I'm bored.   Maybe you should rest.
I'm overweight.   Get a haircut.
I have a toothache.   You'd better hurry.
I'm feeling dizzy.   Why don't you wash it?
I have a headache.   Why don't you eat something?
I have a sore back.   Have something to drink.
I'm not very healthy.   Take some aspirin.
I don't have enough energy.   Take some vitamins.
I'm late.   You could go on a diet.

_____   _____
(another problem)   *(your own advice)*

New Words

Do you know more words ?

Body and health

_____

Listening 📼

1. Easy listening

What should they do? Number the pictures as you listen.

Don't drink any more wine. ❏

Don't lift heavy things. ❏

Find another job. ❏

Quit smoking. ❏

Go on a diet. ❏

Go to bed early. ❏

Lie down. ❏

Put on a sweater. ❏

Take off your shoes. ❏

Stop dancing for a while. ❏

Take a day off. ❏

Take a holiday. ❏

What's the problem? Number the pictures as you listen.

2. Listening task

Listen to the conversation. What is the doctor's advice? What should the patient do? What shouldn't he do? Put a check (✓) in the correct column for each action.

	should do	**shouldn't do**
rest		
work		
take medicine		
drink liquids		
talk		
smoke		

Pair Practice A

Student A look at this page. Student B look at page 52.

Your partner has different pictures. How many of pictures 1, 3, 5, 7, 9 can you identify? Take turns. Tell your partner what you think.

I think number 1 is a …   It could be a …   It might be a …   Maybe it's a …

Answer your partner.

Yes, that's right. *or* No, that's not right. Guess again.

How many guesses do you need for each one?

| 1. | 2. | 3 | 4. | 5. |
| 6. | 7. | 8. | 9. | 10. |

• •

EXTRA! EXTRA!

What can you do with it?

Think of two (or more) uses for each object. Use your imagination. Make a list.

ball	You can (throw) it. You can (kick) it. You can (exercise) with it. You can use it for (a pillow). You can use it for (an earring).

brick	long stick	ball	tire	chopsticks

paper clip	cup	bag	envelope	bowl

7

Social Talk—Problems

1. Listen in

Listen to the conversations.

1.

What's wrong?

I've got a stomachache.

Well, I hope you feel better soon.

Thanks.

2.

How are you feeling?

Not too good. I've got a headache.

Oh, that's too bad. Can I do anything for you?

Can you get me some aspirin?

3.

What's the matter?

I lost my wallet.

Oh, no. Is there anything I can do?

No, I don't think so.

4.

You look upset. Is something wrong?

Yeah, my grandmother died today.

She did? I'm sorry to hear that.

2. Act it out

Work with a partner. Stand up. Act out the conversations. Then make your own conversations. Use your own words and ideas.

Pair Practice B 👥

Student B look at this page. Student A look at page 50.

Your partner has different pictures. How many of pictures 2, 4, 6, 8, 10 can you identify? Take turns. Tell your partner what you think.

I think number 2 is a …   It could be a …   It might be a …   Maybe it's a …

Answer your partner.

Yes, that's right. *or* No, that's not right. Guess again.

How many guesses do you need for each one?

1.   2.   3   4.   5.

6.   7.   8.   9.   10.

• •

EXTRA! EXTRA! 👥

What can you do with it?

Think of two (or more) uses for each object. Use your imagination. Make a list.

You can (throw) it.   You can (kick) it.   You can (exercise) with it.
You can use it for (a pillow).   You can use it for (an earring).

ball

brick   long stick   ball   tire   chopsticks

paper clip   cup   bag   envelope   bowl

Expansion Unit

5

6

7

8

1. Questions and Answers

Match each answer with a question.

Answers	Questions
After I graduate.	Should I buy large or small ones?
At 7:15.	How much rice should I buy?
For two weeks.	How much orange juice should I buy?
I can't. We don't have any bread.	Where is the frozen food?
I didn't buy anything.	Can you make a sandwich for me?
I have an earache.	Is there a pharmacy near here?
I'm going to stay at home.	What did you buy at the market?
It's on Madison Street.	Did you buy some beer?
Please buy the large ones.	Can I help you?
Sorry, I can't. I have to work.	What are you going to do tonight?
Sure. Go ahead.	Where is Chico's house?
It's in Aisle 2A.	When are you going to move to Tokyo?
Two cartons.	What time does the movie start?
Two kilos.	How long will you be in Taiwan?
Yes, I did. I feel terrible.	Can you go to the game with me?
Yes, I did. I got six cans.	What's wrong?
Yes, I'm looking for some socks.	Did you catch a cold?
Yes, there is. It's near the station.	Can I borrow your car?

2. Grammar Watch

Check (✓) the correct sentence, A or B. Circle the errors.

	A	**B**
1.	What she is wearing now?	What is she wearing now?
2.	She's wearing jeans and a green sweater.	She wearing jeans and a green sweater.
3.	Did you invited her to the party?	Did you invite her to the party?
4.	How long you waited for me?	How long did you wait for me?
5.	When did you visit Greece?	When did you visiting Greece?
6.	What you going to do tonight?	What are you going to do tonight?
7.	I'm going to stay at home.	I'm go to stay at home.
8.	I have a headache.	I have headache.
9.	I have go to school tomorrow.	I have to go to school tomorrow.
10.	You should stop smoking.	You should stop to smoke.

3. Language Game—Hot Seat

*One student sits in the hot seat. Other students ask him or her many 'yes/no' questions. Do you …? Did you …? Are you …? Will you …? Are you going to …? Answer **without** saying 'yes' or 'no'.*

Do you live in (Los Angeles)?
I don't live in (Los Angeles).

Is today (Monday)?
Today is (Monday).

How many questions can you answer correctly in two minutes?

4. Vocabulary Game—Opposites

Read each sentence in List A. Find an opposite sentence in List B.

8

List A	List B
I'm trying to lose weight.	I take off my shoes every evening.
How much did you earn?	He is very unfriendly.
I borrowed $10 from her.	We're very unhappy.
I put on my shoes every morning.	This car was cheap.
I think he should wake up.	She always eats dinner at home.
I think she's hard-working.	These two pictures are different.
I'm going to stay up.	I'm going to go to bed.
He is very friendly.	I think he should go to sleep.
She never eats dinner at home.	There's a little rice on the shelf.
This car was expensive.	I'm trying to gain weight.
They are outside the house.	How much did you spend?
There's a lot of rice on the shelf.	I think she's lazy.
These two pictures are the same.	This chair is very comfortable.
This chair is very uncomfortable.	I lent her $10.
They're getting better.	They're getting worse.
We're very happy.	They are inside the house.

5. Interaction Game—Changing Partners

Prepare a card about yourself. Write your name in the middle. In the top left corner, write one word or phrase about your plans for this weekend. In the top right corner, write the name of your favorite place in this city. In the bottom left corner, write one thing that you bought recently. In the bottom right corner, write one word or phrase about your future plans.

Example

Put the card on your desk. Talk to the person on your right. Ask about the things on his or her card.

Tell me about (your plans for this weekend).

Then talk about one of the things on your card. Continue for one minute. Then change partners. Take turns. Talk to at least five people.

First Try

1. Pronunciation

Listen and repeat.

> Do you like rock music?   I love watching old movies.   Do you like it?
> How often do you watch them?   How often do you swim?
> What do you like to do in your free time?   I swim every day.

2. Just listen

Listen to the conversations.

1.

Do you like rock music?
classical music
Yes, I do. Do you like it?
Yes, I do too.

2.

Do you like Chinese food?
American food
No, not really. Do you like it?
No, I don't either.

3.

What do you like to do in your
free time?
I really like swimming.
gardening
How often do you swim?
work in your garden
I do it every day.

4.

What do you like doing in your
free time?
I love watching old movies.
reading comic books
Oh, really? How often do you
watch them?
read them
About twice a week.
almost every day

3. Work in pairs

*Practice the conversations. Then practice again. Use the new words
and phrases.*

Word Bank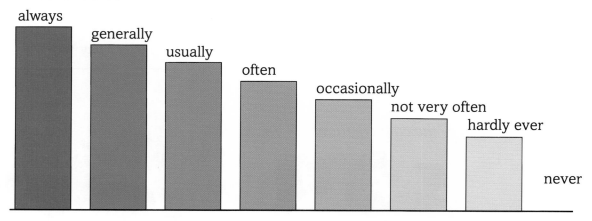

Listen. Repeat the words and phrases.

How often?

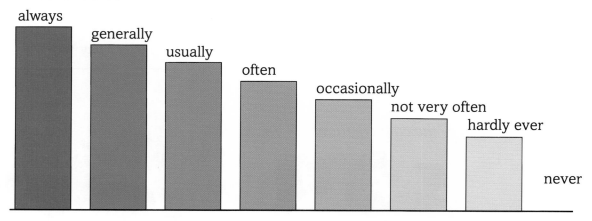

always
generally
usually
often
occasionally
not very often
hardly ever
never

during the summer vacation   during December   during the evening
over the holiday   over the weekend

Activities

Sports and leisure:

hiking   aerobics   gardening   playing soccer

Types of music: classical music
rock   folk   popular (pop)   jazz

Types of television (TV) shows:
quiz show   documentary   comedy
talk show   variety show   drama

Types of food: Mexican   Italian
Japanese   Korean   Chinese
junk food/fast food

Types of books & magazines:
novels   comics   non-fiction
best-sellers

1. Do you like it?

Ask your partner questions. Make a check (✓) for your partner's answers. How many of your answers are the same?

> Do you like (watching football)?
> Yes, I really like it. *or* Yes, I like it a little. *or* No, I don't like it.

	really likes it	likes it a little	doesn't like it
watching football			
playing tennis			
doing aerobics			
watching music videos			
_____ (*Write your own*)			

2. Favorites

Ask your partner:

> What is your favorite (television show)?

free time activity   movie   television show   news program   newspaper
outdoor activity   food   restaurant

3. How often ...?

Ask your partner questions. Make a check (✓) for your partner's answers.

> How often do you (skip breakfast)?   About (once a week).

	often	occasionally	hardly ever	never
stay overnight at a friend's place				
skip breakfast				
sleep less than 5 hours				
_____ (*Write your own*)				

New Words

Do you know more words?

Activities

Frequency (how often)

_____

_____

Listening 🔲

1. Easy listening

Listen to Marcia and Toshi. Have they ever done these things? Make a check (✓) for yes and a cross (✗) for no.

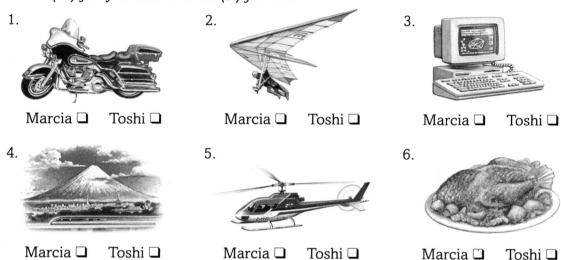

1.   Marcia ❏   Toshi ❏

2.   Marcia ❏   Toshi ❏

3.   Marcia ❏   Toshi ❏

4.   Marcia ❏   Toshi ❏

5.   Marcia ❏   Toshi ❏

6.   Marcia ❏   Toshi ❏

Listen to Meilin and Paul. What do they like? Write 'M' for Meilin and 'P' for Paul under the correct picture.

1.   ❏ Italian food   ❏ Mexican food

2.   ❏ mysteries   ❏ science fiction

3.   ❏ game shows   ❏ sports programs

4.   ❏ rock   ❏ classical

5.   ❏ hiking   ❏ barbecue parties

6.   ❏ science   ❏ history

2. Listening task

Where did they visit? What did they like? Complete the boxes.

Natalie

Place _____

When was she there? _____

What did she like? _____

What didn't she like? _____

Matt

Place _____

When was he there? _____

What did he like? _____

What didn't he like? _____

Sandra

Place _____

When was she there? _____

What did she like? _____

What didn't she like? _____

Pair Practice A

Student A look at this page. Student B look at page 64.

Ask your partner the questions. Record your partner's answers below. Take turns.

Have you ever (tried Thai food)?	Yes, I've tried it.
	or No, I've never tried it.
When did you (try Thai food) for the first time?	I tried it (last year).
What was it like? *or* What did you think of it?	It was good.
	or I didn't really like it.

Have you ever...	Yes/No (✓/✗)	When did you do it for the first time?	What was it like?
1. (try) Thai food?	_____	_____	_____
2. (go) to Australia?	_____	_____	_____
3. (visit) Disneyland?	_____	_____	_____
4. (travel) to London?	_____	_____	_____
5. (visit) Hawaii?	_____	_____	_____
6. (go) sailing?	_____	_____	_____
7. (try) horseback riding?	_____	_____	_____
8. (see) a sumo match?	_____	_____	_____
9. (drive) a truck?	_____	_____	_____
10. (meet) a famous actor?	_____	_____	_____
11. (win) a prize?	_____	_____	_____
12. (ride) in an ambulance?	_____	_____	_____
13. (travel) on a ferry boat?	_____	_____	_____
14. _____	_____	_____	_____
(*Write your own*)			

• •

EXTRA! EXTRA!

Experiences

Which of your partner's experiences are the most interesting? Ask your partner three more questions about his or her 'yes' answers. For example:

Where were you (when you did it)?	Who were you with?
What did you say?	Would you do it again?

Social Talk—Personal News

1. Listen in

Listen to the conversations.

1.

2.

3.

4.

2. Act it out

Work with a partner. Stand up. Act out the conversations. Then make your own conversations. Use your own words and ideas.

Pair Practice B 👥

Student B look at this page. Student A look at page 62.

Ask your partner the questions. Record your partner's answers below. Take turns.

Have you ever (tried Indonesian food)?	Yes, I've tried it. *or* No, I've never tried it.
When did you (try Indonesian food) for the first time?	I tried it (last year).
What was it like? *or* What did you think of it?	It was good. *or* I didn't really like it.

Have you ever...	**Yes/No (✓/✗)**	**When did you do it for the first time?**	**What was it like?**
1. (try) Indonesian food?	_____	_____	_____
2. (go) to Italy?	_____	_____	_____
3. (cross) London Bridge?	_____	_____	_____
4. (travel) by yourself?	_____	_____	_____
5. (visit) Bali?	_____	_____	_____
6. (go) surfing?	_____	_____	_____
7. (try) sky-diving?	_____	_____	_____
8. (see) a boxing match?	_____	_____	_____
9. (go) to a rock concert?	_____	_____	_____
10. (ride) a motorcycle?	_____	_____	_____
11. (fly) in a helicopter?	_____	_____	_____
12. (see) a ghost?	_____	_____	_____
13. (go) to a wedding?	_____	_____	_____
14. _____ (*Write your own*)	_____	_____	_____

● ●

EXTRA! EXTRA! 👥

Experiences

Which of your partner's experiences are the most interesting? Ask your partner three more questions about his or her 'yes' answers. For example:

Where were you (when you did it)?	Who were you with?
What did you say?	Would you do it again?

First Try

1. Pronunciation

Listen and repeat.

> What are you doing?   Can you show me how to do it?   What are you making?   Why don't you stir the eggs?   How do you make it?

2. Just listen

Listen to the conversations.

1.

What are you making?
I'm making curry.
How do you make it?
Can you tell me how to make it?
It's easy. You just sauté the vegetables and add some spices.
put in

2.

What are you making?
I'm making scrambled eggs.
Can I help you?
Can I do anything?
Sure. Why don't you stir the eggs?
mix

3.

What are you doing?
I'm cleaning up.
Can I help you?
Is there something I can do?
Sure. Please put away the newspapers.
Would you mind putting away

4.

What are you doing?
I'm sending a fax.
Can you show me how to do it?
Can you show me how it's done?
Sure. Just dial the number and press
All you need to do is
START.

3. Work in pairs

Practice the conversations. Then practice again. Use the new words and phrases.

Word Bank

Everyday actions

Listen and look at the pictures. Repeat the words and phrases.

| turn on (water/light) | turn off (water/light) | pick up (towel) | put down (towel) | take out (books) | put away (books) |

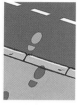   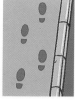  

| cross the street | turn right | turn left | go straight | go past … | stop at … |

| fry | boil | sauté | steam | toast |

| open the can | pour the soup into a pan | add a can of water |

| stir it up | turn on the stove | turn off the heat |

1. What are they doing?

Work with a partner. Ask and answer. Take turns.

What is the man in picture (1) doing?   He's turning on a light.

1.  2.  3.  4.

2. How can I get to ...?

Work with a partner. Take turns.
Make short conversations.

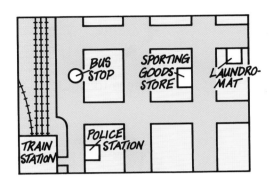

How can I get from the bus stop to
   (the train station)?
It's easy. (Cross the street. Then turn left.)

1. Train Station   2. Laundromat
3. Police Station   4. Sporting Goods Store

3. Series of actions

Work with a partner. Take turns. Say the series of actions.

Here's how to (make soup). (Open the can ...)

1. make tea

2. change a light bulb

Now write your own.

New Words

Do you know more words?

Actions

_____

Listening 🔊

1. Easy listening

Listen. What are they making? Number the pictures.

cheese toast ❑ curry ❑ soup ❑ strawberry ❑
shortcake

coffee ❑ scrambled ❑ popcorn ❑ tea ❑
eggs

Listen again. Check (✓) the verbs that you hear.

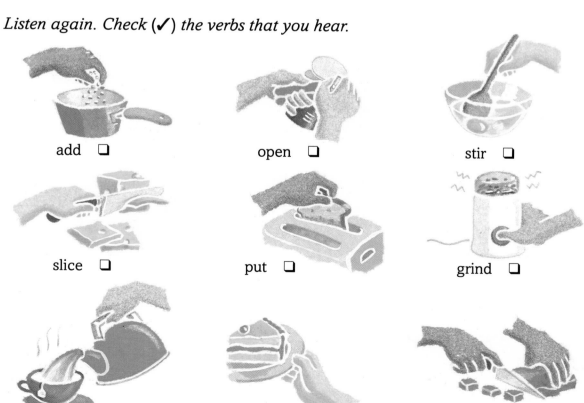

add ❑ open ❑ stir ❑

slice ❑ put ❑ grind ❑

pour ❑ take ❑ cut ❑

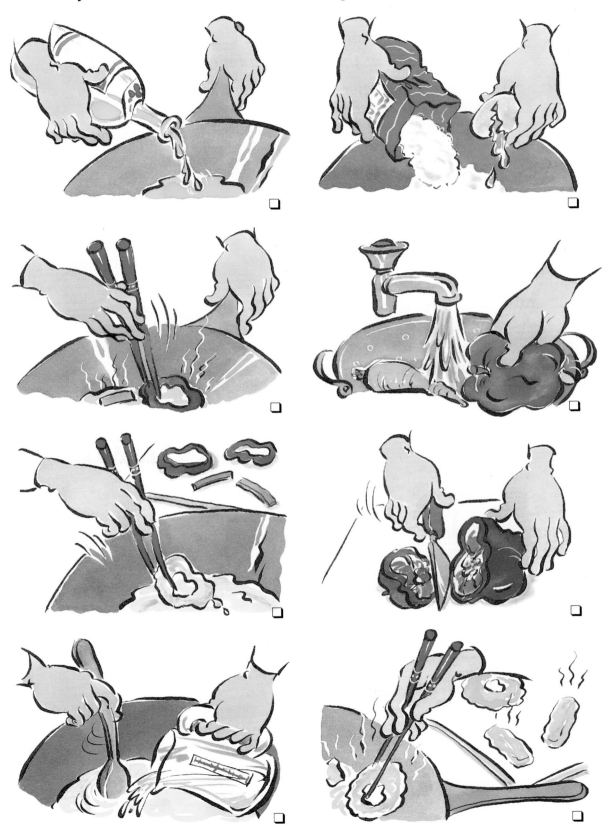

2. Listening task 📼

How do you make it? Listen and number the pictures in the correct order.

Pair Practice A

Student A look at this page. Student B look at page 72.

Your partner has different information. Take turns. Ask your partner this question about 2 and 4:

How do you (use a microwave oven)?   *Number the pictures in the correct order.*

1. Send a fax letter.   2. Use a microwave oven.

1. Put in the letter.
3. Press start.
2. Dial the number.

3. Withdraw money from an ATM.   4. Buy a train ticket from a machine.

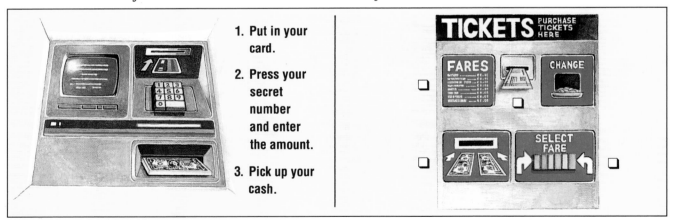

1. Put in your card.
2. Press your secret number and enter the amount.
3. Pick up your cash.

TICKETS PURCHASE TICKETS HERE
FARES
CHANGE
SELECT FARE

• •

EXTRA! EXTRA!

Actions

Choose three of the actions below. Explain and demonstrate how to do each action. Work with a partner.

• put on trousers   • boil an egg   • eat cereal   • wash dishes
• throw a baseball   • mop the floor   • _____ (*Make up your own action*)

10

Social Talk—Apologies

1. Listen in ▭

Listen to the conversations.

1.

Ouch!

Oh, I'm sorry.

2.

Excuse me, I think that's my seat.

Oh, is it? I'm sorry.

3.

I'm sorry I'm late.

What happened?

There was a lot of traffic.

4.

Oh, no. I spilled my drink.

That's OK.

Let me clean it up.

No, don't worry about it.

2. Act it out 👥

Work with a partner. Stand up. Act out the conversations. Then make your own conversations. Use your own words and ideas.

Pair Practice B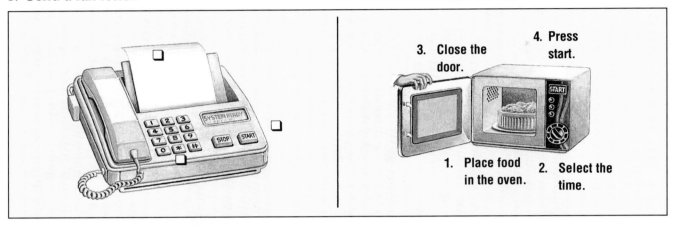

Student B look at this page. Student A look at page 70.

Your partner has different information. Take turns. Ask your partner this question about 1 and 3:

How do you (send a fax letter)? *Number the pictures in the correct order.*

1. Send a fax letter.

2. Use a microwave oven.

3. **Close the door.**

4. **Press start.**

1. **Place food in the oven.**

2. **Select the time.**

3. Withdraw money from an ATM.

4. Buy a train ticket from a machine.

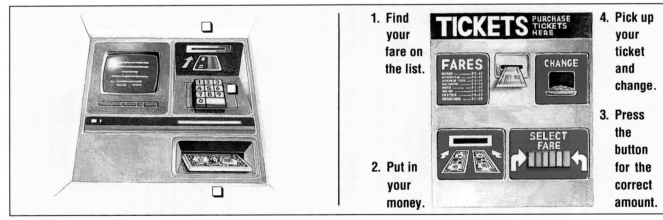

1. **Find your fare on the list.**

TICKETS · PURCHASE TICKETS HERE

FARES   CHANGE

SELECT FARE

2. **Put in your money.**

4. **Pick up your ticket and change.**

3. **Press the button for the correct amount.**

• •

EXTRA! EXTRA!

Actions

Choose three of the actions below. Explain and demonstrate how to do each action. Work with a partner.

- put on trousers
- boil an egg
- eat cereal
- wash dishes
- throw a baseball
- mop the floor
- _____ (*Make up your own action*)

First Try

1. Pronunciation

Listen and repeat.

Should we hire Mr. Perez or Ms. Rijo? I think we should hire Ms. Rijo. Because she's more experienced.	Should we live in New York or Los Angeles? I think we should live in Los Angeles. Because the weather there is better.

2. Just listen

Listen to the conversations.

1.

Should I vote for Clint Reston or
(name)
Regina Lawson?
(name)
I think you should vote for Regina Lawson.
(name)
Why?
Because she's more experienced
more honest
than Clint Reston.
(name)

2.

Should I become an English teacher
a doctor
or a businessperson?
a lawyer
I think you should become an
English teacher.
(occupation)
Why do you think so?
Because teaching is
practicing medicine
more interesting than selling.
more rewarding   practicing law

3. Work in pairs

Practice the conversations. Then practice again. Use the new words and phrases.

Word Bank

Listen and look at the pictures. Repeat the words and phrases.

About people

cheerful   funny   honest   intelligent   interesting

lazy   nervous   quiet   shy

About things

It's bad (worse, the worst)   It's boring (more boring, the most boring)   It's bright (brighter, the brightest)

It's more … the most …

comfortable   convenient   dangerous   difficult (to learn)   easy (to use)

exciting   interesting   modern   popular   useful

1. He's ... She's ... They're ... It's ...

Complete each sentence. Use these words:

| interesting | funny | shy | useful | easy to use | comfortable |

1. She always tells jokes. She's very _____.
2. Tom never talks in class. He's very _____.
3. These tools can be used for many things. They're very _____.
4. I like sitting in this chair. It's so soft. It's very _____.
5. I don't like this movie. It's not very _____.
6. Even children can use this machine. It's very _____.

2. It's more ... than ...

Work with a partner. Take turns to compare each set of items. Say one sentence about each.

Apples are (smaller) than watermelons.
Motorcycles are (more dangerous) than bicycles.

1. the country and the city
2. Japan and the USA
3. dogs and cats
4. football and swimming
5. English and your language
6. _____
   (*Write your own*)

3. He looks ... She looks ...

Work with a partner. Take turns to describe these people.

The person in number (1) looks (more interesting) than the person in number (2).
The person in number (3) looks like the (friendliest) person.

1.
2.
3.

New Words

Do you know more words?

About people

_____
_____
_____

About things

_____
_____
_____

Listening

1. Easy listening

Listen. Circle the expressions you hear.

Elizabeth

quiet

shy

intelligent

kind

generous

James

outgoing

serious

loud

funny

Dorothee

active

energetic

creative

nervous

happy

Linda

interesting

exciting

cheerful

friendly

David

intelligent

nervous

talkative

Millie and Max

warm   selfish

generous   funny

hard-working

friendly

not so friendly

Listen. Check (✓) 'likes' or 'doesn't like' for each activity.

	likes	doesn't like	
1.			tennis
2.			running
3.			aerobics
4.			coffee
5.			beer
6.			whisky

2. Listening task

Listen. Which do they prefer? Circle the item. Why do they prefer it? Write one word or expression.

1.

tea   coffee

_____

2.

American food Japanese food

_____

3.

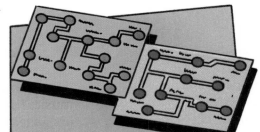

Green Line   Blue Line
(subway lines)

_____

4.

large classes small classes

_____

5.

gas oven microwave oven

_____

6.

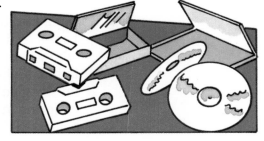

tapes   CDs

_____

7.

German cars Japanese cars

_____

8.

diamonds   pearls

_____

Pair Practice A

Student A look at this page. Student B look at page 80.

Your partner has different information. Ask your partner these questions:

> What is (Kevin) like?
> What does he like to do?

Who would be the best for each other? Why?

> I think … and … would be a good match because …

 Kevin  Clark  Eric  Martin

1. Amy

I'm an active person. I really like jogging and aerobics. I usually exercise every day. I work for an insurance company. I'm an office manager. I like to take fun vacations.

2. Heather

I'm sort of an academic person. I like art and classical music. I often go to art galleries and art shows. I have a job at a travel agency as an assistant manager.

3. Neesha

I'm a traditional person. I want to find a man who will be a good father. Right now, I'm finishing college. I'm majoring in business, because I think it's important to be practical.

4. Chieko

I'm kind of international. I moved to the U.S. five years ago. I work at a restaurant every day from 5 o'clock until midnight. I feel really free here. I don't want to get married and have a family. That's not for me.

· ·

EXTRA! EXTRA!

I think so, too.

Work in pairs. Find three things that both you and your partner like. Also find three things that you and your partner don't like. Ask questions about food, schedule, favorite activities, lifestyle, opinions.

> Do you like (swimming)?   Yes, I do. *or* No, I don't.
> I like it, too. *or* I don't like it, either.

Social Talk—Talk between Friends

1. Listen in

Listen to the conversations.

1.

> You like playing golf?
>
> Yes, I do.
>
> So do I.
>
> Hey, that's great! Let's play together sometime.

2.

> Where are you going?
>
> To Colorado.
>
> Are you going to ski?
>
> Yeah, I am.
>
> Well, have a nice time.

3.

> Hi, Meg. What are you doing?
>
> I'm watching the Monday Night Movie.
>
> Can I join you?
>
> Sure.

4.

> It's been good knowing you.
>
> Yeah, I hope to see you again soon.
>
> Well, see you.
>
> Bye.

2. Act it out

Work with a partner. Stand up. Act out the conversations. Then make your own conversations. Use your own words and ideas.

Pair Practice B

Student B look at this page. Student A look at page 78.

Your partner has different information. Ask your partner these questions:

| What is (Amy) like? |
| What does she like to do? |

Who would be the best for each other? Why?

| I think … and … would be |
| a good match because … |

 Amy    Heather    Neesha    Chieko

A. Kevin

I'm interested in a lot of things. I moved to the U.S. seven years ago. I like it here. I work for an airline company, usually in the evenings from 4 o'clock to midnight. I don't want a family right now.

B. Clark

I'm a salesman for a big car company. I like to do things. I belong to a sports club, and I often swim and lift weights. I like to go on long skiing vacations and on scuba-diving trips.

C. Eric

I'm a painter. I'm not so successful now, but I think that someday my paintings will be well-known. Someday, if I have enough money, I would love to visit Asia.

D. Martin

I have my own business. I'm very successful. I'm divorced. I want to marry again but I must find a very traditional woman. I like to save my money.

•••

EXTRA! EXTRA!

I think so, too.

Work in pairs. Find three things that both you and your partner like. Also find three things that you and your partner don't like. Ask questions about food, schedule, favorite activities, lifestyle, opinions.

| Do you like (visiting art galleries)? | Yes, I do. *or* No, I don't. |
| | I like it, too. *or* I don't like it, either. |

Expansion Unit

1. Social Talk Review

Can you remember these dialogues? Complete the missing information.

1.

Hi, Mari.
*Hi, Richard. Richard, I'd like you
_____ Jason.*
Hi, Jason. Glad to _____.
Glad to _____, Richard.

2.

What _____
the concert?
I thought it _____!

3.

Can I _____?
No, thanks. I'm _____.

4.

Hi, Tom. _____ the
new Spike Lee movie with us?
No, I can't tonight. Thanks _____.
Sure.

5.

_____ wrong?
I've got a _____.
Well, I hope you _____.
Thanks.

6.

_____ what?
What?
We're both in class 1-A.
Oh, really? _____

7.

Oh, no. I spilled my drink.
That's OK.
_____ clean it up.
No, don't _____ .

8.

Hi, Meg. What _____?
I'm watching the Monday Night Movie.
Can I _____?
Sure.

2. Vocabulary Consolidation

Word Categories

How many words do you know for each category?

1. **Daily activities**
   get dressed
   _____
   _____

2. **Interests**
   cycling
   _____
   _____

3. **Family members**
   father
   _____
   _____

4. **Clothes**
   _____
   _____
   _____

5. **Food items**
   _____
   _____
   _____

6. **Containers**
   _____
   _____
   _____

7. **Places**
   _____
   _____
   _____

8. **Directions**
   _____
   _____
   _____

9. **Aches**
   _____
   _____
   _____

3. Grammar Game

Comparing

Play in a group of three or four. One person points to two items of the same color. The other players must make a comparison. Take turns.

(Madonna) is more/less (popular) than (Michael Jackson).
(Madonna) is (taller) than/isn't as (tall) as (Michael Jackson).
Both of them are (pop stars).
Neither of them is (a politician).

office	car	panda	Madonna
pizza	school	Katharine Hepburn	carrot
pencil sharpener	snake	apples	home
Whoopi Goldberg	CD player	elephant	milk
dog	Michael Jackson	coffee shop	television

4. Interaction Game

Find someone who ...

Stand up. Walk around your class and ask questions. Find someone for each question. Ask them to write their name on the line.

Who was born in the same month as you? _____

(*name*)

Who was born on the same day (of the month) as you?

_____

(*name*)

Who has the same number of brothers or sisters as you?

_____

(*name*)

Who has the same favorite singer as you? _____

(*name*)

Who learned two languages as a child? _____

(*name*)

Who has seen a crime? _____

(*name*)

Who has a child? _____

(*name*)

Who has written a book? _____

(*name*)

Who has met a famous person? _____

(*name*)

Who has been to San Francisco? _____

(*name*)

5. Opinions

Work with a partner. Which item from each set of three do you like most? Why? Say one sentence. Take turns.

I like (parrots) best because they are (beautiful).

1.	pop	folk	rap
2.	swimming	aerobics	jogging
3.	snakes	lizards	spiders
4.	dogs	cats	parrots
5.	rainy weather	snowy weather	sunny weather
6.	morning	afternoon	evening
7.	yellow	green	blue

Add your own:

8. _____   _____   _____

6. Mini-speech

Work in a group of four. Each person should choose one of these topics:

1. *A person I like*
2. *One of my favorite activities*
3. *One time when I was nervous*
4. *An interesting travel experience*

Think of three facts or ideas about this topic. Make short notes:

Topic: A person I like – Lillian
personality – funny, warm
interesting
things we do together –
travel, watch movies, talk

Talk to your group members about your topic for one minute. Then each member of the group should ask one question about your topic. Then the next person should talk for one minute. Continue until everyone has had a turn to talk.

Classroom Notes

These Classroom Notes will help the teacher make the classroom more active and more communicative, and make the students' learning more enjoyable and more effective. For a more complete teaching guide, please consult the Teacher's Manual.

These notes are divided into two sections: Teaching Procedures and Unit Notes.

Teaching Procedures

Each section in *Prime Time English* is designed for 30–60 minutes of classroom work. For most classes, each unit will require about three hours of class time.

First Try:

 ### 1. Pronunciation Practice

Model the phrases or play the tape. Have the students repeat the phrases, first chorally, then individually. Pay attention especially to stress and intonation.

 ### 2. Modeling the Dialogues

Say the lines in the four presentation conversations, or use the tape.
Have the students follow along in their books, or, if they are able, without looking in their books.

 ### 3. Class Practice

The students work in pairs. One student is the first speaker in each dialogue; the other student is the second speaker in the dialogue. The students should face each other and make eye contact as they practice. After finishing the dialogues, the students change roles.

4. Acting

The students create their own dialogues, based on the patterns and illustration given, and present them in front of the class. This brief acting exercise helps students to internalize the forms they have practiced. It will also help you check student performance.

Word Bank:

 ### 1. Presentation

Play the tape in which the narrator pronounces the words in short phrases and sentences, or narrate the pictures and words yourself. Say the words in the picture as the students point to the pictures and repeat the words. The purpose of this step is to insure general comprehension of the word meanings.

2. Repetition

Ask your students to repeat key words. Ask questions about the picture. (You may wish to have an enlarged photocopy of the page for this purpose.)

 ### 3. Active Practice

The Word Bank exercises, on the facing page, require the students to actively process the words. Different exercises call for different groupings. Most can be done in pairs, as this will encourage maximum oral work. Demonstrate the first one or two items in each exercise and then allow the students ample time to complete the exercise before checking it.

4. New Words

Students should select words that are new to them and write them down in the New Words box. Ask each student to write down five (or more) new words—words he or she individually would like to learn and remember. You may also ask students to write out illustrative sentences or use some other memory aid. You may also elicit questions from the students about related words that are not on the Word Bank page that they would like to learn.

Also encourage your students to keep Vocabulary Cards. On each card they should write one new word. They should study these regularly and set goals for their own vocabulary learning—such as learning ten new words per week.

Easy Listening:

 ### 1. Presentation

Play the tape two or three times, or until nearly all of the students can discriminate between the forms (that is, can get the answers correct).

2. Checking

Check the answers. To check the answers, you can simply call out the correct answers orally (**1** b, **2** a, etc.). Once all the students have checked their answers, replay the taped exercise so that the students can confirm the correct answers. This can be a very useful form of feedback.

Listening Task:

1. Warm Up

Look at the illustration with the students. Ask questions about the picture and the people in it. This will help the students build expectations for listening.

 ### 2. Listening

Play the tape and have the students try the listening task. You may wish to stop the tape after each item, to check comprehension or to replay the segment.

3. Follow Up

Check the answers. Find out if the students misunderstood any parts of the tape or task and retry those sections.

Pair Practice:

1. Preview of Language

Model expressions appear at the beginning of each Pair Practice to show to the students the kinds of expressions they will need to do this exercise with language accuracy. Model these expressions and explain any unknown vocabulary or grammar. The students should repeat each sentence.

 ### 2. Modeling

Students are to work with a partner. A students must look at the A page only; B students must look at the B page only. Each exercise involves a basic information gap: A and B must exchange information in order for them to accomplish the goal of the task. Be sure that the students understand this procedure. Have two volunteers begin the exercise while the other students watch and listen. If necessary, have the whole class act as the A student for number 1 and take the role of the B student yourself.

3. Free Practice

Allow ample time for all of the students to practice the activity and to complete the task. Give a time limit to make the outcome more important and to focus the students' attention on meaning.

4. Extra! Extra!

The Extra! Extra! activity at the bottom of the page is an open-ended speaking practice. You may have the students who finish early go directly to this exercise, or you may allot time for all students to try it.

5. Checking

Check that the students have completed the task. Ask questions and review the key grammar points. If time permits, try a Follow Up activity.

Social Talk:

1. Listening

Have the students listen to the tape as they read the cartoon bubbles. You may wish to have the students repeat the lines. Point out to the students any features of the situations that are of interest. Elicit from the students any questions they might have.

2. Oral Practice

Have the students practice the situations in pairs. Each student should practice both parts of the conversations. After the students have practiced, some of the student pairs can present their conversations to the whole class.

Unit Notes

These Unit Notes provide suggestions for Warm Up and Follow Up activities to accompany each section of every unit.

Introduction Unit (pages vi–viii)

This unit can be used in your first class meeting and periodically throughout the first few weeks of your course. The Introduction Unit consists of nine sets of items for the students to learn through listening and repetition.

1. Letters of the alphabet
Follow Up:
Call out some place names (Tokyo, Seoul, Taipei, Los Angeles). Ask the students to spell them aloud.

2. Numbers
Follow Up:
Say some simple arithmetic problems to the class (9 plus 7, 20 minus 8). Ask them to say the answers.

3. Colors
Follow Up:
Point to some items in the room. Ask: *What color is it?* Call out names of other items (such as lemon, ocean, pine tree). Ask the students to say what color(s) it is.

4. Time
Follow Up:
Use two pencils (or other long, thin objects). Hold up the two pencils to show different clock times (for example, both pencils pointing up is 12:00). Make several different times. The students should say the times.

5. Days and months
Follow Up:
Ask several students: *When is your birthday?* or *When is (name of holiday)?*
Also say the date of a national or international holiday (for example, July 4th). Ask the students: *What holiday is this?*

6. Years

Follow Up:
Ask some questions: *When was (famous event)?* Then ask the students to try asking you some questions like this.

7. Dates

Follow Up:
At the start of every class day, ask one student to write the date on the board: Day, Month, Year.

8. Directions

Follow Up:
Name some items in the classroom. Ask the students to describe where they are. Or state some locations (for example: *It's in the corner of the room, near the door).* Ask the students: *What is it?*

9. Classroom Expressions

Follow Up:
Make a large poster with these expressions on it. Post it in the front of the class. Every time a student needs to use one of the expressions, point to the expression on the poster.

UNIT ONE (pages 1–8)

Objectives:
Present and practice language related to personal interests and daily activities.

Visuals:
If possible, bring in additional materials to class related to the themes of introductions, daily activities, and personal interests. For example, you may want to bring in—or ask your students to bring to class—cut-out pictures of popular pastimes. Post these around the room with key words and phrases written on cards beneath the pictures.

First Try (page 1)

Warm Up: Role cards
Make several large role cards which show name, residence, and job. For example, one role card might read: John Adams, Tokyo, English Teacher. Hold one of these cards in front of you for the class to read, and say: *Hello, I'm _____. I live in _____. I'm a _____.* Then give another one of the cards to a volunteer and elicit the same three sentences.

Follow Up: Introductions
After the activity, continue the role cards activity. This time, have the students circulate and introduce themselves to at least five other people. For each person, they should ask: *What do you do?* and *Do you like your job?*

Word Bank (pages 2–3)

Warm Up: Everyday activities
Bring in some pictures of people engaged in basic everyday activities (such as eating breakfast, taking a bath, riding a commuter train). Hold up one picture, covered with a white page. Slowly, reveal the picture to the class. Who can guess first what the action is? Write the actions on the board.

Follow Up: Vocabulary expansion
To give more practice with using the vocabulary words, ask several students in the class the questions in Exercises 2 and 3. You may want to expand this list also by adding other possible activities (go to the school cafeteria, do English homework, take the train during rush hour).

Easy Listening (page 4)

Warm Up: Jobs
Before playing the tape, ask the students to identify each job in both grids. Ask the students: *What does this person do?* Accept all possible answers.

Follow Up: Vocabulary quiz
Ask the students questions orally about the vocabulary. Examples: *What do you call someone who*

coaches a basketball team? (A basketball coach) Where does a loan officer work? (At a bank) What does a newscaster do? (Announce the news)

Listening Task (page 5)

Warm Up: Possible answers

Before playing the tape, ask the students for possible answers to these questions: *What is her present job? (What do you think her current job is?) What previous jobs has she had? (What do you think her previous jobs were?) What do you think her interests are?* Accept all possible answers.

Pair Practice (pages 6 and 8)

Warm Up: Jobs review

Review the jobs and the actions of each job in the Word List. Be sure to model the questions: *What does _____ do? Where does _____ live?*

Follow Up: Famous people

Check the Extra! Extra! activity with the whole class. If possible, bring in additional pictures of famous people (in arts, music, entertainment, politics, sports) to test your students.

Social Talk (page 7)

Warm Up: Pictures

Have the students look at the pictures. Ask some questions about the pictures: *Who is introducing whom?*

Follow Up: Party

Tell the class to pretend they're at a party. Ask all of the students to stand up and introduce at least three other people to their classmates. They should use the three different expressions from the model dialogues.

UNIT TWO (pages 9–16)

Objectives:

Practice giving and understanding descriptions.

Visuals:

If possible, obtain some additional materials related to the theme of description. For example, you may post around the room pictures of unusual-looking people (various hair styles and clothing). To reinforce vocabulary learning, put small word cards below each picture.

First Try (page 9)

Warm Up: Questions

Write these two questions on the board: *What does _____ look like? What's _____ wearing?* Ask these questions about several students in the class. Elicit answers about age (*in her mid-twenties*), body type (*tall*), hair (*long, dark hair*), clothing (*wearing blue jeans*).

Follow Up: Original dialogues

Ask for volunteer pairs to come to the front of the class to perform original dialogues based on number 1 and number 2. You may wish to write the dialogue frame on the board so that they do not need to carry their textbooks.

Word Bank (pages 10–11)

Warm Up: Preview

Ask the students how many of the words they already know. You may wish to quiz them by asking them to cover up the words and answer your questions, such as: *What is number 1?*

Follow Up: Clothes

To give more practice with the vocabulary, continue Exercise 3 as a whole class exercise. You can ask several additional questions, based on what your students are actually wearing today.

Easy Listening (page 12)

Warm Up: Anticipation

Before playing the tape, elicit simple descriptions from the students: *What are the people in the top left square wearing?* etc. This will help build anticipation for what the students will hear on the tape.

Follow Up: Description
Choose a picture (for example, top left). Ask the students to describe it.

Listening Task (page 13)

Warm Up: Picture ID
Since many of your students may not be familiar with the directions, you may wish to demonstrate with a large picture of a group of people. Tape it to the board, write names around the picture, and describe the people in the picture. Ask one student volunteer to draw arrows from the names to the people as you describe them.

Follow Up: My family
Ask all of your students to bring in a picture of their family or a group of friends. In small groups, have the students describe the people in their picture.

Pair Practice (pages 14 and 16)

Warm Up: Similar pictures
Draw two similar pictures on the board, using a room with simple items in it (cups, glasses, tables, chairs, windows, doors). Make four or five small positional differences between the pictures. Ask the students: *What's different?* Make a list of the items that are different. (For example: *The chair is next to the door/next to the window.*) This will prepare the students for the upcoming pair activity.

Follow Up: Changes
Ask a group of five students to stand in front of the room. Then have the other students look away while the five students rearrange their positions. Can the other students describe the changes?

Social Talk (page 15)

Warm Up: Where are they?
Have the students look at the pictures. Point to each picture. Ask this question about each picture: *Where are they?*

Follow Up: In your language
Ask your students: *Do you know any similar expressions to "He's great", "It was so-so", "It was fantastic!", "I'm glad you like it"? Do you have expressions like these in your native language?* (For each situation) *What do you say in your native language?*

UNIT THREE (pages 17–24)

Objectives:
Activate vocabulary for actions, emotions, and time expressions.
Practice question and statement forms in past tense.
Practice formulaic language for future events (Social Talk).

Visuals:
If possible, have your students make collages of daily activities or job-related actions. Post these around the room, with the main verb beneath. You can use these to quiz the students on past forms of verbs.

First Try (page 17)

Warm Up: Personal news
If you know something about the students' personal schedules, begin by asking some personal questions, such as *How was your (meeting) yesterday?* Respond to the news: *That's great* or *That's interesting* or *That's too bad.*

Follow Up: Responses
Write these responses on the board: *That's terrific. I'm glad to hear that. That's too bad. I'm sorry to hear that.* Ask the students to think of news to elicit each response. For example: *There's no class tomorrow. It's going to rain tomorrow. I'm going to get married.*

Word Bank (pages 18–19)

Warm Up: Yesterday
Ask the students: *What did you do yesterday?* Ask the students to list as many activities as they can remember. Write the verb phrases on the board for everyone to see.

Follow Up: Emotions
Write several "emotion" words on the board (*angry, surprised, sorry*). Make up a few very short anecdotes (for example: *I was riding on the train this morning, and a man pushed me out of my seat.*). At the end, say: *I felt...* Can the students say the "emotion" you felt?

Easy Listening (page 20)

Warm Up: Differences
Ask the students to look at the pictures of the faces. Can they describe the emotions? (For example: *In number 1, one man looks happy; one man looks sad.*) This will help the students anticipate what is on the tape.

Follow Up: Weather
Write these expressions on the board: *sunny, rainy, foggy, cool, humid, windy, snowy, calm, clear.* Ask questions such as: *What's the weather like today? What is the weather usually like in (place or time)?* to check the students' understanding.

Listening Task (page 21)

Warm Up: Postcards
Bring in any postcards you have from different places. Hold up a postcard and ask: *Does anyone know where this is from?* Say something about each postcard or make up a very short letter for each one. Read this aloud to the class.

Follow Up: Recall
Have your students close their books. Ask some questions about Lisa and Ted. For example: *Where did Ted go? What did Ted do there? What happened to Lisa in the London airport? Did her parents lend her some money?*

Pair Practice (pages 22 and 24)

Warm Up: Realia
Bring in several bits of "realia" to help prepare the students for this activity. Possible items include: a dish, a computer disk, a running shoe, a box of tissue paper, a camping knife, a sponge. Write this question on the board: *What did I do yesterday?* Hold up each item and elicit possible answers: *You washed dishes. You ate at a restaurant. You had a snack.* Be sure that your students use past tense forms. After you have elicited three possible answers, go on to the next item.

Follow Up: Past actions
Continue the Extra! Extra! game with the whole class. See how many activities most people in the class did yesterday. You can make this more challenging by excluding actions in school since most students do many of the same actions while at school.

Social Talk (page 23)

Warm Up: Picture study
Before playing the tape, ask questions about each picture: *What are they talking about?*

Follow Up: Presentations
Allow several pairs to present their conversations to the class. Encourage them to take their time—to speak slowly and clearly, with the proper emphasis.

UNIT FOUR: EXPANSION UNIT (pages 25–28)

This is an expansion unit to review and consolidate grammar, vocabulary, and language functions. There are reviews of short conversations and the grammar of questions and answers. There is also a vocabulary game and an interaction activity.

Questions and Answers (30 minutes)
This exercise may be done individually, in pairs, or as a whole class. Have the students read one item in the answer column first. Then they are to think of a question for this answer. After they think of a possible question, they should try to find that question, or a similar one, in the question column.

Correct this exercise by having the students write both the questions and the answers on the blackboard. As you correct the exercise, note the kinds of errors that are often made. Make a point of reviewing these items and giving additional quizzes on them during the course.

Follow Up: Short answers
Continue this activity orally. Give a short answer (for example, *No, I don't.*). The students are to ask a question that will give that answer (for example: *Do you smoke? Do you live in New York?*).

Grammar Watch (15 minutes)
This exercise may be done individually or in pairs. Have the students check (✔) the correct sentence and circle the error in the incorrect sentence. This will help raise the students' awareness of the underlying grammar point.

Follow Up: Errors game
Identify the grammar items in this quiz that your students have most trouble with. For each item, make two similar index cards, one with an error. Post the cards side-by-side on the board. Have the students come to the board and remove the card with the error.

Description (25 minutes)
This exercise can be done in pairs, with each student contributing one sentence. The students should challenge themselves to make as many meaningful sentences as possible about each picture.

Check this exercise as a whole group activity by eliciting individual sentences from the students. Be sure that all of the students understand what other students say.

Follow Up: Scenes
You can expand this activity by bringing in photographs of currently popular movies. Have the students describe each photograph in the same way.

Vocabulary Exercise—Categories (25 minutes)
This exercise can be done individually or in pairs. The challenging aspect of the activity is to state why one item does not fit.

Check this exercise by asking: *Which one doesn't belong and why?* Write this frame on the board to help the students answer: *(Item) doesn't belong because it (reason).*

Follow Up: Odd one out
You can expand this game by having each student write four items on a strip of paper. Three items should be related in some way; the other should be the odd one which does not fit with the others. Collect the slips. Read them aloud. Can the students identify the odd one and give a reason for excluding it?

Vocabulary Expansion (30 minutes)
This exercise is a review of many of the vocabulary groups from Units 1–3. To make this into a game, provide a time limit (suggested: 10 minutes) and see who has the highest total. (The students may go beyond the suggested numbers of items.)

When checking the exercise, spend only a minute or so with each group of items.

Follow Up: Word Bank review
Use this opportunity to remind the students to review their Word Bank pages. Ask individual students what new words they wrote on their Word Bank pages. Encourage them to write these words on small cards to review regularly.

Interaction Game—One–Minute Pantomime (20 minutes)
Allow each pair of students at least ten minutes to prepare and rehearse their skit—either before or during class. In large classes, not all pairs will be able to perform their skit, so you may wish to have the students work in groups of four or six, so that each pair can do their own skit for a smaller group.

The language practice in this activity comes from trying to recall each action in order and using past tense and sequence markers (*first, next, after that*, etc.).

You can make this into a written review exercise by having the students write out the sequence of actions of the skits.

Follow Up: Video Skits
Show a short scene from a video program, with the sound off. Have the students recall the actions in the skit.

UNIT FIVE (pages 29–36)

Objectives:
Practice functional language related to shopping.
Learn to distinguish between count and non-count nouns; learn quantifiers for non-count nouns.
Complete tasks using quantities and prices.

Visuals:
If possible, bring in advertisements from supermarkets, which often show the containers (package, box, etc.) and generally show the price. Look at the items on the Word Bank pages for ideas. You may also want to bring in large, full color pictures of different food items.

First Try (page 29)

Warm Up: Shopping trip
To set the tone for food and shopping language, ask several students what they bought recently (yesterday) at the grocery store. Follow up by asking: *How much (how many) did you buy?* Write the items and the quantities on the board.

Follow Up: Supermarket
Make a quick sketch of a supermarket on the board. Label the aisles (Aisle 1A, 1B, 2A, 2B) and the front and the back of the store. Write the names of some grocery items in the aisles. Tell the students they are the supermarket clerks. Ask one student: *Excuse me. Do you sell (bread)? (Yes, we do.) Where is it? (It's in Aisle 2A.)* Then have the students ask you the same kinds of questions.

Word Bank (pages 30–31)

Warm Up: Food items
Write the following categories on the board: Fruit, Vegetables, Dairy Products, Meat, Fish, Snack Food. Have several markers (or pieces of chalk) available. Ask the students to come up to the board and write as many items as they can think of under each heading.

Follow up: Containers game
To provide extra practice with containers, play this simple game. Say: *We need some (rice, apples, coffee,* etc.*).* The students (or student you name) should say: *We'd better buy some.* You respond: *How much (many) should we get?* The student must answer with a correct counter (e.g. *one kilo*) or container (*one bag*).

Easy Listening (page 32)

Warm Up: Containers
Before playing the tape, ask the students to say the items in the grid. They should use counters or containers, for example: *(There's) a bag of potato chips.*

Follow Up: Food items
Play this as a game. Ask one student to begin a sentence: *I'm going to buy (one bag of)...* Another student has to finish the sentence and then begin another: *...potato chips. I'm also going to buy two cans of...* Continue until all students have a turn.

Listening Task (page 33)

Warm Up: Picture preview
Ask the students to look at each picture. Ask: *What kind of store is this? What can you buy at this kind of store?*

Follow Up: What do they want?
Play the tape an additional time and ask what the customer wants in each store.

Pair Practice (pages 34 and 36)

Warm Up: Advertising
If possible, bring in advertising sections of a newspaper. Find two stores (for example, electronics shops) that sell the same goods. Place these ads on the board. Ask some students to come up and find the "Best Buy" for different items. This will prepare them for the activity in this pair practice section.

Follow Up: Brand names
Using the advertising section of a newspaper, or your own memory, make a list of famous

manufacturers or brand names for various items (cars, bicycles, computers, clothes, perfume, etc.).
Say the name; the students try to answer with the item. (For example, you say: *IBM*. The students
answer: *Computers*.)

Social Talk (page 35)

Warm Up: Picture preview
Have the students look at the pictures. Ask some questions about the pictures: *Where are they?*
What does the customer want?

Follow Up: Restaurant
Try a role play activity, with one waiter or waitress and two customers. Provide a brief menu to
help guide the activity. You may add some element of conflict to make the situation more
challenging (for example, the restaurant is out of some items on the menu; or some items on the
menu are very unusual; or the waiter is very busy and the customers are very slow).

UNIT SIX (pages 37–44)

Objectives:
Practice use of verb forms to express future actions.
Learn new vocabulary related to times, places, directions.

Visuals:
If possible, bring to class some additional materials related to future plans and activities. Post these
around the room with a brief caption for each.

First Try (page 37)

Warm Up: Activities
Write this question on the board: *What are you going to do* _____ *?* Using different time
expressions (*after class, tonight, this weekend*), ask several students individually. Be sure that your
students answer with: *I'm going to...*

Follow Up: Original dialogues
Ask for volunteer pairs to come to the front of the class to perform original dialogues based on
dialogues number 1 and number 2. You may wish to write the dialogue frame on the board as a
reminder.

Word Bank (pages 38–39)

Warm Up: Cities and towns
Bring in some photographs of city and small town scenes. Ask the students what they can identify
in each picture. Write the key words on the board.

Follow Up: Local map
To extend the practice from Exercise 3, bring in a large local map and ask several questions: *How
do I get to...?* Encourage your students to answer with full forms.

Easy Listening (page 40)

Warm Up: Future actions
Ask your students to describe each picture, using a future form: *He's going to go on a diet*, etc. You
can prompt them by asking the question: *What is he going to do?*

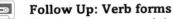

Follow Up: Verb forms
Play the tape a second time. Ask the students to note down the verb forms (*going to, have got to,
want to*) and the time expressions that the speakers use.

Listening Task (page 41)

Warm Up: Verb expressions
To help your students anticipate some of the language in this long extract, write the key
expressions (see Tapescript) on the board and have the students pronounce them.

Follow Up: Summer plans
Write several verb phrases on slips of paper. These should be activities someone might do during a
summer vacation (visit my relatives, see the Grand Canyon, go to Disneyland). Put these slips on a

table in the room. Ask each student to find five activities they would like to do during the summer. Then ask each student to describe their summer plans.

Pair Practice (pages 42 and 44)

Warm Up: Predictions
Bring in several bits of "realia" to help prepare the students for this activity. Possible items include: a ticket, a cup of laundry soap, a colander (or other item for cooking), a graduation cap, an envelope, a video tape, a ski glove. Write this question on the board: *What am I planning to do this weekend?* Hold up each item and elicit possible answers: *You're going to a concert. You're planning to go to a movie. You're going to see a play.* Be sure that your students use future forms. After you have elicited three possible answers, go on to the next item.

Follow Up: Fortune teller
Have your students work in groups of five. Each person writes a fortune (prediction) for every other person in the group. Then each student collects and reads his or her fortunes. Which ones did the student hope for?

Social Talk (page 43)

Warm Up: Picture preview
Have the students look at the pictures. Ask some questions about the pictures: *Where are they? Who is inviting whom? What is the event?*

Follow Up: Invitations
Have each student make a mock diary for the coming week with two or three events in it (concerts, plays, parties, etc.). Ask the students to walk around the class inviting others to go with them. They should write the names of other students who accept their invitations. Remind them to use the invitation forms from the Social Talk conversations.

UNIT SEVEN (pages 45–52)

Objectives:
Practice functional language for requests, invitations, and excuses.
Learn vocabulary related to health and sickness.
Practice use of modals.

Visuals:
If possible, bring in visuals related to health care. Post these around the room. Put some simple advice phrases (for example: *Be sure to get enough rest.*) beneath the pictures.

First Try (page 45)

Warm Up: Invitations and excuses
Write these two headings on the board: *Invitations* and *Excuses.* Under *Invitations,* write *go to a movie, go to a restaurant, have coffee.* Under *Excuses,* write *have to work, have to study, have to take care of my mother.* Go around the class, inviting some students to an event (*Min, would you like to have coffee with me after class?*). The students should give a "no" answer and an excuse. (*I'm sorry, I can't. I have to work today.*)

Follow Up: Original dialogues
Write these two words on the board: *invitation* and *excuse.* Ask for volunteer pairs to come to the front of the class to perform an original dialogue. Each dialogue should have an invitation to do something (for example, play tennis) and an excuse (for example: *I have to work. I have a sore back.*).

Word Bank (pages 46–47)

Warm Up: Health vocabulary
To introduce some of the health vocabulary, ask some questions to the whole class and give some advice or consolation: *Does anyone have a cold today? (Oh, I'm sorry to hear that. I hope you feel better soon.) Does anyone have a headache? (Maybe you'd better take it easy today!)*

Follow Up: Red tape
Give the students small strips of red tape (or red ribbon). Ask them to put the tape on any parts of their body where they have had an injury in the past. (Some people will ask for many strips!) Then

ask individual students: *What happened here?* The students should try to give a brief story to tell what happened.

Easy Listening (page 48)

Warm Up: Advice
Write these phrases on the board: *Maybe you should... Maybe you could...Why don't you... Maybe you'd better...* Then state several problems: *I don't like my job. I'm gaining too much weight. I'm working too much recently.* Ask the students to give you advice, using these expressions.

Follow Up: Reasons
Write these expressions on the board: *It's too... I'm not _____ enough.* Then make several statements that require reasons, such as: *I can't understand this book. (It's too difficult. I'm not smart enough.) I can't eat hot curries. (They're too hot.) I can't drink this coffee. (It's not hot enough.).* Can the students make up reasons?

Listening Task (page 49)

Warm Up: Ask the doctor
Introduce the activity by asking the students: *What advice does a doctor give you if you have a cold?* Write the advice on the board. Underline phrases that show advice (*should, ought to, had better, must, have to*).

Follow Up: Advice
Ask the students to think of some everyday problems (such as aches and pains, busy schedules, arguments with friends or co-workers). Ask the students to write out each problem on a strip of paper. Collect the strips and distribute them to different students. Other students should write advice for the problem on the back. Collect the problems and the advice. Read out some of the most interesting ones.

Pair Practice (pages 50 and 52)

Warm Up: What is it?
Take several photographs (magazine cut-outs will work) and cover them with a sheet of white paper. Slowly, pull up the white page to reveal the photo. Who can guess what it is? *It might be... Maybe it's a... I think it's a...* Explain to the students that this type of guessing game is the main activity in the Pair Practice section.

Follow Up: List of ideas
Compile the list of uses for each object in the Extra! Extra! activity. Many students will be surprised at the creative ideas of their classmates.

Social Talk (page 51)

Warm Up: Problem talk
Ask the students what kinds of problems people often talk about. They may mention health problems, money problems, family problems, social problems, environmental problems. Ask: *When someone tells you about a personal problem, what can you do? (Show sympathy? Give advice?)*

Follow Up: In your language
Ask questions such as these to find out what the students may know about usage of English: *Have you ever heard these expressions? (What's wrong? What's the matter? I'm sorry to hear that. etc.) When? Do you know any similar expressions?* Ask questions such as these to find out about cross-cultural similarities: *Do you have expressions like this in your native language? Do you use them in the same way (as shown in the illustrations)? If not, how is your native language different?*

UNIT EIGHT: EXPANSION UNIT (pages 53–56)

This is an expansion unit to review and consolidate grammar, vocabulary, and language functions. There are reviews of short conversations and the grammar of questions and answers. There is also a vocabulary game and an interaction activity.

Questions and Answers (30 minutes)
This exercise may be done individually, in pairs, or as a whole class. Have the students read one item in the answer column first. Then they are to think of a question for this answer. After they

think of a possible question, they should try to find that question, or a similar one, in the question column.

Correct this exercise by having the students write both the questions and the answers on the blackboard.

Follow Up: Short answers
Continue this activity orally. Give a short answer (for example: *No, I don't.*). The students are to ask a question that will give that answer (for example: *Do you smoke? Do you live in New York?*).

Grammar Watch (15 minutes)
This exercise may be done individually or in pairs. Have the students check (✓) the correct sentence and circle the error in the incorrect sentence. This will help raise the students' awareness of the underlying grammar points.

Follow Up: Errors game
Identify the grammar items in this quiz that your students have most trouble with. For each item, make two similar index cards, one with an error. Post the cards side-by-side on the board. Have the students come to the board and remove the card with the error.

Vocabulary Game—Opposites (25 minutes)
This exercise can be done individually or in pairs. It is best for the students to read one sentence (for example: *He's trying to lose weight*) and then try to think of an opposite sentence. After thinking of an opposite, the student then looks for this sentence in List B.

Check this exercise by having the students write the pairs of opposite sentences on the board.

Language Game—Hot Seat (20 minutes)

Being in the "hot seat" means being under pressure. However, this activity should feel like a game, rather than seem like a test. To prepare for the game, have everyone write down two or three yes/no questions that they can ask their fellow students. When the game begins, they should take turns saying their questions. The person in the hot seat should try to answer quickly, without saying yes or no. Keep track of the number of questions each student can answer before slipping with a yes or no answer. It is best not to correct grammar during this exercise, as it is intended to promote fluency. If you hear an ungrammatical question or answer, you may simply repeat it using correct grammar.

Interaction Game—Changing Partners (30 minutes)
Make an example card shape on the board. Go through the card preparation with the students: write your name in the middle of the card, a word or phrase about your weekend plans in the upper left corner, the name of your favorite place in the city in the upper right, and so on. Allow ample time for each student to prepare a card. Walk around the class to make sure everyone has completed this step.

Demonstrate the activity by having the students ask you about one of the words or phrases on your card. Encourage them to use expressions such as: *Tell me about (visiting your sister)*. Use one or two sentences to answer. For example: *I'm going to visit my sister on Sunday. She lives in _____*. Then indicate that the students should ask you a question about another item on your card.

When the students understand the procedure, have them work in pairs to do the same. Change partners several times.

UNIT NINE (pages 57–64)

Objectives:
Practice functional language used for expressing likes and dislikes, agreement and disagreement.
Practice present perfect tense for talking about experiences.
Learn new vocabulary related to interests and activities.

Visuals:
If possible, bring in pictures of unusual activities (e.g. sky-diving). Post these around the room with the caption: *Have you ever...?*

First Try (page 57)

Warm Up: I do too
Write some of the Activities vocabulary (such as hiking, classical music, Italian food) from the Word Bank on the board. Point to one and ask a student: *Do you like...?* Respond: *I do, too* or *I don't, either.* Try to generate several short conversations like this.

Follow Up: Things we like
Write this sentence frame on the board: *I like _____ ing _____.* Have several markers (or pieces of chalk) available. Ask the students to come to the board and write several sentences using this frame. Afterwards, read out the sentences. Can the students guess who wrote each one?

Word Bank (pages 58–59)

Warm Up: Examples
Before the students open their books, write the headings for Activities (sports and leisure, types of music, types of television shows, etc.) on the board. Elicit from the students as many examples as possible of items for each heading.

Follow Up: Both of us
Write this sentence frame on the board: *Both _____ and I like _____.* Ask the students to volunteer sentences, based on what they found out about their partners in Exercises 1, 2, and 3.

Easy Listening (page 60)

Warm Up: Survey
Before listening, take a brief survey of the students, using the items from the exercise: *How many people have ever driven a motorcycle? How many of you have ever gone snow camping?* etc.

Follow Up: Agree?
Think of two or more popular musicians, entertainers, movies, books, foods. Write them down on the board. Ask two students to be contestants. Continue the game show from the listening exercise. For each category, ask one of the students: *Do you like _____ ?* And then ask the other. When the second student agrees with the first, he or she should answer: *I do too* or *I don't either.*

Listening Task (page 61)

Warm Up: Where is it?
Ask your students to look at the illustrations. Where are these places? Have any of your students been there? If so, what did they like? What didn't they like?

Follow Up: Personal trip
Ask your students to think about an interesting trip they have taken. Ask them to write down the place, when they were there, what they liked, what they didn't like. Ask several students about their trips.

Pair Practice (pages 62 and 64)

Warm Up: Clippings
Look through a recent newspaper or news magazine to find a story about an unusual or daring experience someone has had. Clip out the article. Hold it up while you explain briefly what it is about. Explain that this Pair Practice is about your own unusual experiences.

Follow Up: How was it?
Ask for volunteers to talk about one of their experiences, as suggested in the Extra! Extra! activity. Ask each volunteer a few questions only (for example: *What was it like? How did you feel?* etc.) and then go on to the next person.

Social Talk (page 63)

Warm Up: Picture preview
Before playing the tape, ask questions about each picture: *What are they talking about? Is it good news or bad news?*

Follow Up: In your language
Ask questions such as these to find out what the students may know about usage of English: *Have you ever heard these expressions? (Guess what? Congratulations!) When? Do you know any similar expressions in English?* Ask questions such as these to find out about cross-cultural similarities: *Do you have expressions like this in your native language? Do you use them in the same way?*

UNIT TEN (pages 65–72)

Objectives:
Practice use of imperative forms of verbs.
Increase active use of vocabulary to describe sequences of action.
Learn language for giving directions.

Visuals:
If possible, bring in some "how to" instruction manuals with visuals of steps involved in different projects. Some examples are home improvement manuals, repair manuals, exercise manuals (aerobics, yoga, etc.). Post some pictures around the classroom, with verbs beneath the pictures.

First Try (page 65)

Warm Up: How do you use it?
To set the tone for this unit, bring in some props such as a tape player, camera, pencil sharpener, hand-held computer game. Ask a volunteer student to come to the front and explain how to use each object. Use expressions like: *What are you doing? How do you do it? Can you show me how to do it?*

Follow Up: Performance
Ask some pairs of students to perform one of the dialogues, using props. They can improvise, but they should mention all of the important steps in the process.

Word Bank (pages 66-67)

Warm Up: Memory
Ask the students to look at the page for one minute. Then have them close their books. How many actions can they remember? Write down the actions on the board.

Follow Up: Series of actions
Expand this list of actions by writing down some everyday series of actions, such as: *getting into a car and starting it, washing your face, putting on your shoes, making a cup of tea, buying something from a vending machine.* Ask one student to demonstrate the action, without words. Stop the student at each step and ask the class: *What is she (he) doing now?* Write the new verb on the board, making a series of the actions.

Easy Listening (page 68)

Warm Up: Recipe
Prepare some original recipe directions, or use the first one or two items in the Tapescript. Give the directions one sentence at a time. After each sentence, ask the students: *Do you know what the recipe is for?*

Follow Up: Follow the actions
Name one of the directions (for example, making tea). Ask for a volunteer to start the directions as she or he imitates the action. Let other volunteers complete the sequence.

Listening Task (page 69)

Warm Up: Favorite foods
Ask the students what foods they know how to make. Make a list of these foods on the board. See if any students mention tempura, which is the topic of this listening task. If so, ask them to see if this recipe is similar to their own.

Follow Up: Favorite recipes
Have the students work in pairs. One student explains a favorite recipe while the other writes out the main steps. Collect the recipes. Read some of them out to the class.

Pair Practice (pages 70–72)

Warm Up: Modern machines
Write the names of the four machines used in this pair practice on the board (fax machine, microwave oven, ATM, ticket machine). Ask the students for examples of other modern machines. Write them on the board also.

Follow Up: Step-by-step
Continue the Extra! Extra! activity with the whole class. Ask for a volunteer to give you step-by-step

directions on how to wash your face. Follow the directions very exactly in order to encourage the students to give more accurate instructions.

Social Talk (page 71)

Warm Up: Apologizing
Ask the students to think of all the situations they can in which you might need to apologize to someone. Make a list on the board of at least ten situations.

Follow Up: In your culture
Ask the students if they think apologizing is different in their country and in another country (e.g. the United States). Ask for examples.

UNIT ELEVEN (pages 73–80)

Objectives:
Practice use of comparative forms.
Learn new adjectives for use in comparisons.
Practice giving reasons for opinions.

Visuals:
If possible, bring in pictures suggesting comparisons: two or more people in the same picture, two or more animals, appliances, rooms, cities, etc. Pair these pictures and post them around the room.

First Try (page 73)

Warm Up: Two people
Write two names on the board or hold up two pictures of different people. Ask the students to make any comparisons they can. Write the comparative forms on the board, noting the difference between one-syllable adjectives (e.g. taller than) and multisyllabic adjectives (e.g. more attractive than).

Follow Up: Reasons
Ask several "advice" questions to the students: *Which _____ do you think I should _____?* For example, *Which restaurant should I go to for lunch — Burger Palace or Super Taco?* Ask the students to give you a reason (*Because _____ is more _____ than _____.*).

Word Bank (pages 74–75)

Warm Up: Preview
Ask the students which of the adjectives on the page they already know. Write these on the board. Then point to one adjective and ask: *Who do you know who is _____?* or *What do you know that is _____?* Elicit as many answers as possible.

Follow Up: Comparisons
Bring in three photographs of well-known people. Post these on the board. Ask the students to make comparison sentences, as they did in Exercise 3.

Easy Listening (page 76)

Warm Up: Prediction
Before playing the tape, ask the students to look at each picture. Can they predict which adjectives will be used? Ask: *What do you think Elizabeth is like?*

Follow Up: Preferences
Expand the list of items in the second part of the exercise. Use current entertainers and activities. Ask several students to state whether they like or dislike the items on the list.

Listening Task (page 77)

Warm Up: Preview
Preview the items. As you do this, ask the students if they think one of the items is better than the other. Encourage them to give reasons.

Follow Up: Recall
After completing the exercise, ask the students the reasons the speakers gave for their preferences. (*It's milder... It's lighter...* etc.)

Pair Practice (pages 78 and 80)

Warm Up: Marriage partners
Write this sentence on the board: *For a marriage partner, I'd choose someone who _____*. Ask the students for examples of ways to complete this sentence.

Follow Up: Three things
Ask the students about the Extra! Extra! activity. Ask several different pairs of students what three things they and their partners like and don't like.

Social Talk (page 79)

Warm Up: Questions
Ask questions about each picture: *Where are they? What are they doing?*

Follow Up: Talk among friends
Ask the students if they have heard conversations like this among friends. Ask: *What topics do friends often talk about?* and *What activities do friends often do together?*

UNIT TWELVE: EXPANSION UNIT (pages 81–85)

This is an expansion unit. There is a Social Talk review, a vocabulary review, a grammar review, two interaction games, and a short speech activity.

Social Talk Review (30 minutes)

This is a selective review of all of the Social Talk sections from the book. Allow the students to work in pairs to recall the dialogues. After they have attempted the review, they may turn back to the original pages to check their answers.

Follow Up: Functions
Replay several taped dialogues for the Social Talk sections. Ask the students to identify the functions of the conversations (greeting, invitation, apology, etc.).

Vocabulary Consolidation (30–60 minutes)

You may wish to assign this for homework and check it during the following class. Note that there are many possible completions for each list.

Follow Up: Connections
On a large sheet of paper write out about 20 related vocabulary words from the book. Have the students draw lines to words that are connected to each other in meaning.

Grammar Game—Comparing (20 minutes)

This activity should take on a game-like quality if you encourage creative comparisons between the items. Substitute other items or expand by providing additional, local names.

Interaction Game—Find Someone Who... (15 minutes)

This is a popular group interaction game which encourages practice of question forms. Be sure that the students record their answers by having the other students write their names on the lines.

Opinions (20–40 minutes)

Do this exercise in two stages. First, have the students work in pairs to give their opinions on each set of items. Then, go through the list with the whole class, encouraging volunteers to give their opinions.

Mini-speech (20–30 minutes)

This activity works best when the students have time to prepare and use notes to give their speeches. (They should refer briefly to their notes only, not read from them.) If possible, have the other students involved by filling out a speech report or by asking questions after each student's speech is finished.

Follow Up: Video presentations
Video tape (or audio tape) the student presentations. Have each student transcribe his or her own presentation and make comments on how to improve the next presentation.

Acknowledgements

I would like to thank the many individuals who assisted me in the course of developing of *Real Time English* and *Prime Time English*:

Damien Tunnacliffe for his initial vision and direction
Tim Hunt for his encouragement during the planning stages
Gill Negus for her direction in the production stages
Helena Gomm for her steady attention and enduring vigor throughout the project
Eden Temko for her clarity and amiable humor during the final stages of editing
The Design Department, especially Nicola Witt and Helen Locker (Design Locker), and Neil Adams (D.P. Press) for their creativity and aplomb in designing the books
The Art Editors, Hilary Fletcher, Marilyn Rawlings and Veena Holkar, and the Production Controller, Donna Wright
David Briscoe and the A-V department for their resourcefulness in producing the tapes
The staff of the American English department at Longman Group UK, particularly Louise Elkins, and to the other publishers and editors, especially Nicola Gooch, who helped give life to the books.

Shinsuke Suzuki of Longman Japan, for his valued personal and professional guidance
The staff of Longman Japan, particularly Hiromi Tsuchiya, Steve Martin, Steve Galloway, Hideki Komiyama, and Takashi Hata for their congenial support
Kevin Bergman for his wise counsel on the project from start to finish.

Dugie Cameron of Longman Asia Pacific for his insistence on inclusiveness and high standards of development
Joanne Dresner and Debbie Sistino of Longman Publishing Group in the USA for their valuable input on many aspects of the project
Many others within the Longman Group worldwide, particularly Jill Wang and Jung Ja Lee, for their openness and generosity in offering suggestions.

Valerie Randall for her wit and sharp conceptual ability in developing the dialogues

The teachers who reviewed or piloted earlier versions of the books in their classes, for furnishing clear feedback and suggestions on ways to improve them:

Harumi Adachi
Rudi Besikof
Carmen L. Casagnanos
DeWitt Conklin
Teresa Cox
Tomoko Fujita
Nobuko Hara
Ken Hartmann
Marc Helgesen
Junko Kurata
Ken Kitazawa
Chris Lynch
Hiromi Matsumoto
Mariko Miura
Sian Munekini
Mie Okada
Jeremy Palmer
J. Saul Ray
Leslie A. Rice
Cheryl Richmond
Hung-En Seng
Izumi Seo
David Shaw
Eric Strickland
Hisae Suzuki
Miho Takagi
Yoichi Takagi
Junko Tanikawa
Keiko Thompson
Tom Werner

My family, Keiko, Ammon and Leon Rost, for helping me with numerous bits of language research, and for providing the humor, warmth, and sustenance needed during this marathon.

M.R.

We would like to thank the following for their permission to reproduce photographs:

Ace Photo Agency, pages 38 post office (Mark Stevenson), 83 snake (C.T.H.Smith) and 83 television (Vibert Stokes); Anthony Blake Photo Library, page 83 apples (Graham Parish); Britstock IFA pages 6 and 8 translator, 75 left (Forster), 75 centre (Fred), 83 car and dog (both Schmidbauer); BT Pictures, page 43 below left; Colorific, page 38 hospital (Don Hunstein) and school (Alon Reininger/Contact Press); Ronald Grant Archive, page 26 except below right; Tony Hertz, page 38 movie theater; Image Bank, pages 6 and 8 police officer, doctor, lawyer, tour guide, flight attendant and photographer, 38 campus (Steve Dunwell), library (Sobel Klonsky), town (Giuliano Colliva), mountain (Steve Satushek), lake (Stockphotos Inc/Robert E. Burdick), river (Barrie Rokeach), 43 below left inset, 83 panda (Nevada Wier), pizza (Nino Mascardi) and home (David W. Hamilton); Life File Photographic Agency, pages 6 and 8 athlete; The Moviestore Collection, page 26 below right; Photo Researchers Inc, pages 38 bank (John Spragens Jr), hairdresser (Eunice Harris) and 83 office (Benelux); Pictures Colour Library, pages 38 school and train station and 83 CD player; Retna Pictures, pages 6, 8 and 90 Sinead O'Connor (Chris Taylor), 38 park (J. Acheson), 83 Madonna and Michael Jackson (both Phil Loftus); Rex Features, pages 6 and 8 Woody Allen, Andre Agassi, Alain Prost and Whoopi Goldberg, 83 Katherine Hepburn (Sipa Press/John M. Mantel) and Whoopi Goldberg; Tony Stone Worldwide, pages 6 and 8 musician and writer, and 83 elephant (Chris Harvey); Telegraph Colour Library, page 75 right (Tony Ward); Zefa Picture Library (UK), page 11 left and centre (both Norman) and right (Wartenberg).

The photographs on pages 50 and 52 (compact discs) were taken by John Birdsall; pages 23, 43 except below left, 51 except below right, 63 and 79 by Gareth Boden; pages 7, 15, 35 and 71 by Peter Lake; pages 34, 50, 52 (except compact discs), 83 (carrot and pencil sharpener) by Longman Photographic Unit; pages 38 (bus stop and bus station), 51 below right, 83 (milk and coffee shop) by David Sanford.

Illustrated by Richard Adams, Noel Ford, Neil Gower, Bill Gregory, Pauline Hazelwood, Tim Kahane, Maggie Ling, Frances Lloyd, Colin Mier, Jonathan Satchell, Sharon Scotland and Bob Warburton.

Cover illustration by Rosemary Wood

Longman Group UK Limited
Longman House, Burnt Mill, Harlow, Essex CM20 2JE, England and Associated Companies throughout the world.

First published 1994

Set in 12/13.5pt Monotype Amasis by DP Press Limited, St Julians, Sevenoaks, Kent TN14 0RX

Produced by Longman Singapore (Pte) Ltd
Printed in Singapore

ISBN 0 582 09222 1